Brat Life

ALSO BY CAREN J. TOWN
AND FROM MCFARLAND

*LGBTQ Young Adult Fiction:
A Critical Survey, 1970s–2010s* (2017)

*"Unsuitable" Books: Young Adult Fiction
and Censorship* (2014)

*The New Southern Girl: Female Adolescence
in the Works of 12 Women Authors* (2004)

# Brat Life

*Growing Up Military
in Fiction and Nonfiction*

CAREN J. TOWN

McFarland & Company, Inc., Publishers
*Jefferson, North Carolina*

ISBN (print) 978-1-4766-7696-8
ISBN (ebook) 978-1-4766-5131-6

LIBRARY OF CONGRESS AND BRITISH LIBRARY
CATALOGUING DATA ARE AVAILABLE

Library of Congress Control Number 2023057533

© 2024 Caren J. Town. All rights reserved

*No part of this book may be reproduced or transmitted in any form or by any means, electronic or mechanical, including photocopying or recording, or by any information storage and retrieval system, without permission in writing from the publisher.*

Front cover image: © Jacob Lund/Shutterstock

Printed in the United States of America

*McFarland & Company, Inc., Publishers
Box 611, Jefferson, North Carolina 28640
www.mcfarlandpub.com*

To my siblings, Brian Town and Ila Friend,
for joining me (albeit inadvertently) in Brat life
and for staying with me after it ended.
To my stepchildren—Megan McLinn and Brendan,
Adam, and Matt Perkins—who were Navy Brats.
I hope you find yourselves reflected in these pages.
And for my Brat friends, especially John Woiton
and my former student Megan Flanery,
I acknowledge what you're feeling, I applaud
your sacrifice, and I thank you for your service.

# Acknowledgments

For the fourth time, I would like to acknowledge the support Georgia Southern University has given me over the years through academic leave, the generous encouragement of my colleagues, and my fantastic department chair, Beth Howells. I would like, once again, to give a shout out to my students, who have always been my inspiration and my source of intellectual support during these recent dark times. I'd also like to acknowledge my brilliant therapist, Amanda Rickard, Psy.D., who has helped me uncover many of the insights about Military Brats shared in this book. I would also like to acknowledge my daughter, Rosa Town, who contributed to editing this book, partly out of a desire to better understand her Military Brat mother. Finally, many thanks and much love to my husband, Patrick J. Perkins, retired Senior Chief in the U.S. Navy, for all the moral support, laundry, shopping, and meals he has provided over the years it took to finish this book.

Most importantly, I'd like to acknowledge all the Military Brats out there, whose honesty about the challenges they experienced while ensconced in the Fortress of military life have provided inspiration and information for this study. I hope I can do justice to the ways in which you have been tried and found to be strong, resilient, and optimistic despite what you've been through. Your service is rarely, if ever, acknowledged, and I hope this book is a small step toward doing just that.

# Table of Contents

*Acknowledgments*   vi
*Preface*   1
*Introduction: Looking Inside the Walls of the Fortress*   3

**One.** "I rarely give up my vigilance, and I have no idea what it is I am waiting for": Book-Length Autobiographies   15

**Two.** "Blanket of risk": Shorter Autobiographical Narratives   45

**Three.** "Our fathers are military officers first, and fathers second": Young Adult Novels of Brat Life   57

**Four.** "Military brats don't have hometowns": Adult Novels About Brat Life   88

**Five.** "A Secure Base": Famous Brats and Their Life Stories   123

*Conclusion: "Warriors [and Their Families] Have a Right to Reclaim Their Lives": The Price We Pay and the Solutions We Can (But Do Not) Offer*   149

*Bibliography*   159
*Index*   163

# Preface

This book began the day I was born in Wiesbaden, West Germany, the first child of a Lieutenant in the United States (U.S.) Army and his Army wife. He chose the military as his career when he applied to West Point, and she chose him. I did not choose my parents or the world in which they were going to raise me, but every aspect of my childhood and young adulthood was shaped—for better and for worse—by the military. My father was deployed to Vietnam (twice) and came home with symptoms of PTSD that would last, untreated, for the rest of his life. My mother suffered her own private hell, caused, in part, by the strains of moving and trying to maintain a household with an often-absent husband. My sister and brother, who also experienced much of their childhoods as Army Brats, had their share of troubles. This included a brief stint in Iran followed by a hasty exit when tensions between the American-backed government of the Shah began to crumble under revolutionary pressure. In short, every aspect of my family's lives from 1955 (when my father graduated from the Academy) onward was shaped by the pressures of military life.

The seeds of this book were planted when I read Mary Wertsch's *Military Brats*. Wertsch showed me that my family's experiences (and my own) were by no means unique—that they were part of a culture that encourages secrecy, fortitude, and commitment to a higher good. After devouring Wertsch's book, I realized that I was not alone in feeling adrift, unable to connect with those people who had grown up in the same city in which they were born, who had lifelong friends that they saw regularly, and who had a sense of home, of belonging. The research I have done on the autobiographies, biographies, and fictional

## Preface

renderings of Military Brats has been an attempt to connect with my tribe, to understand our shared experiences and traumas, and to try to imagine how the lives of the children of America's servicemen and servicewomen might be improved in the future.

As I began my research, I found that there were a few well-known accounts of the lives of Military Brats, in particular the harrowing stories of Pat Conroy and the equally disturbing stories of Sarah Bird and Elizabeth Berg. I also discovered there were several young adult novels about Brat life ranging from hilarious to deeply troubling. However, what I did not find, other than in Wertsch's book, were studies on the psychology of military life or systematic critical analyses of the kinds of writing—both fictional and nonfictional—of that life; nor did I find analyses of recurrent tropes and themes. In short, very little has been written about the lives of these children, who number in the hundreds of thousands and who are often ignored in the policy-making arms of the military. Although things have improved since I was born into Brat life, it remains important to give those children, who did not enlist in the services or enroll in the military academies themselves, a voice.

Consequently, this book will first consider the collective mental health of Military Brats, using Wertsch's book as a touchstone, then move to the compelling (and often surprisingly funny) autobiographies of those kids. It will continue to novels and short stories written for both young adult and adult audiences about Brat life, and it will end with the biographies of four famous Brats. Ultimately, I hope to offer a glimpse into a narrative for Brats that is both hopeful for their futures and respectful of their sacrifices.

# Introduction
## *Looking Inside the Walls of the Fortress*

> The military brats of America are an invisible, unorganized tribe, a federation of brothers and sisters bound by common experience, by our uniformed fathers, by the movement of families being rotated through the American mainland and to military posts in foreign lands. We are an undiscovered nation living invisibly in the body politic of this country. There are millions of us scattered through America, but we have no special markings or passwords to identify each other when we move into a common field of vision.
> —Pat Conroy, "Introduction," *Military Brats*, xvii

Children born to families in which at least one parent is in the military are known, in military circles, as "Brats"—Army Brats, Navy Brats, Air Force Brats, and Marine Brats. Although several branches of the service have tried, over the decades, to come up with less pejorative names (such as "Navy Juniors" for the children of Naval officers or after-the-fact positive acronyms such as "Bold, Resilient, and Tenacious" or "Bold Responsible Adaptable Tolerant"), this tribe of military children, for the most part, thinks of itself as Brats, and therefore it is the term of art for any discussion of their experiences, beliefs, values, and challenges. This somewhat amorphous and certainly itinerate class of children is, unsurprisingly, given the peripatetic nature of their lives and the need for secrecy surrounding their parents' careers, one of the least studied and most insular of groups of children in the

## Introduction

United States. Their experiences have rarely been chronicled, unlike the stories of their parents, who have seen both their adventures and their traumas replicated in books, songs, and movies. Recent television shows like Lifetime's *Army Wives* (2007–2013) have shifted the focus to the experiences of military spouses, and the 2020 HBO series *We Are Who We Are* attempts to tell the story of Brats stationed overseas. However, detailed factual or fictional accounts of the lives of the children of warriors are difficult to find, and these children mostly remain unknown and uncelebrated.

According to statistics gathered from the United States Department of Defense in 2014, almost two million children live in military families, and in 2012, "the largest proportion—approximately 37 percent or 730,000 children—were zero to five years old" (Osofsky and Chartrand 62). These children live in families that "move on average every two to three years within the United States or overseas" (Guzman 9). In addition, more than two million military personnel, almost half of them parents, were sent to serve in war zones in Iraq and Afghanistan between 2001 and 2015 (Wadsworth, Bailey, and Coppola 23). Thus, U.S. Military Brats move often, sometimes as frequently as every year. Their parents are deployed to war zones, on the ground, on ships and on submarines, and to other places where children are not allowed. The lives of their military parents are often kept secret from them, and yet they are charged with the same mission of duty, honor, and country as their serving parents, despite never having enlisted themselves. These children serve in their own ways and are, at the very least, affected materially and psychologically by the dislocations, dangers, and high expectations of military life. They grow up without permanent homes, have little contact with extended families, and fear the very real threat of death and injury to one or both of their parents. Consequently, they often have difficulty creating and sustaining relationships and frequently go through their entire lives not sure where or if they belong.

This matters to civilians, or it *would* matter if people were aware of it, because these children experience disruptions, confusions, and traumas that are rarely addressed by the wider society. This is the very society to which most Military Brats will return after their

*Introduction*

18-year "tours of duty" end once they age out of military dependency. According to a 2014 study, the "frequent relocations disrupt children's schoolwork, activities, and social networks, requiring their ongoing adjustment to new schools and cultures" (Guzman 9). This constant adjustment and readjustment can create long-term psychological consequences. In addition, "parental deployment can affect the physical health, academic performance, behavior, family life, mood, and anxiety level of military children" (Guzman 9). Not knowing whether one's father or mother will be injured, or die, is bound to play a role in a child's mood or behavior. Multiple deployments, which were common during the Iraq and Afghanistan wars, "may increase the risk that young children will be maltreated" (Osofsky and Chartrand 61). This can take the form of neglect, parentification, and/or abuse.

During these increased deployments of recent years, military families "have also experienced more spousal depression, anxiety, and parenting stress, as well as a heightened sense of ambiguous loss. All of these may limit a parent's emotional availability, putting children at greater risk for emotional and behavioral problems" (Osofsky and Chartrand 62). Many of these children will be resilient and cope well, especially with support from their caregivers, peers, and the military community. However, for some, "disruptions in primary relationships and support systems can hamper social and emotional development" (Osofsky and Chartrand 64), and many will suffer both neglect and abuse, as well as the stress of living in a conflict-laden family environment. Despite these circumstances, these distressed and traumatized children will attend schools with civilian children, play on their sports teams, socialize with them, and enter adulthood alongside them.

For Brats whose parents are not deployed, life can be equally stressful. Although, given the nature of enlistment requirements, at least one parent will have completed high school and earn a salary and benefits "that compare favorably with similar civilian occupations" (Wadsworth, Bailey, and Coppola 24), Military Brats have to cope with the chronic stressors of military life such as "the demands of military jobs, which can include long hours and intrusions into family life" (Wadsworth, Bailey, and Coppola 24). Even when family members

# Introduction

are not deployed, the activities associated with military life, "such as training, peacekeeping, patrolling air and sea, and responding to natural disasters at home and abroad" (Wadsworth, Bailey, and Coppola 24), provoke ongoing anxiety in the lives of Brats.

In particular, the psychological effects of being part of the continual preparation for war and the threat of injury or death during deployment can be profound. Being separated from parents "can challenge the foundations of secure attachment relationships, competent emotion regulation, and other abilities needed for successful functioning later in life" (Wadsworth, Bailey, and Coppola 24). Since 2001, more than 50,000 American service members have been physically wounded, more than 6,500 have died, and as many as 400,000 have incurred so-called invisible injuries, including traumatic brain injuries, post-traumatic stress disorder, depression, and anxiety (Wadsworth, Bailey, and Coppola 24).

Military children are "28% more likely to have carried a knife or gun to school, and 23% more likely to have had suicidal thoughts" and "reported more risky behavior than civilian children, including more use of cigarettes and other substances, and more experiences of violence and harassment" (Wadsworth, Bailey, and Coppola 24). These rates, including those for suicidal thoughts, behavior disorders, and need for psychotropic medications, rise when children experience the deployment of a parent and increase further when the parent is injured or killed in combat (Wadsworth, Bailey, and Coppola 25). This is not to say that the children of military parents will likely become school shooters or commit suicide, but that school systems and larger communities should pay closer attention to the particular needs of these children in order to keep all members of society safe.

These challenges do not affect school-aged children alone. In "The Preschool Child and the Military Family," Charles R. Privitera emphasizes that "it is the social stresses inherent in military life which disrupt the continuity and emotional stability of the family that are most disruptive for the preschool child. More specifically, it is the episodic experience of transient father absence which has the most pathogenic effect on the child's evolving personality" (5). Having fathers (and increasingly these days, mothers) absent for some (or perhaps even all)

*Introduction*

of a young child's early years can affect the child's personality development in profound and perhaps life-altering ways.

Given that most military children attend school and extracurricular activities with civilians, even if they live on military bases, psychological stress and resulting maladaptive behaviors can have implications for the wider communities in which they live (and which benefit financially from the infusion of money generated through the Department of Defense's Impact Aid funding). A community may well want the economic boon provided by military bases indirectly (and military children directly), but it also needs to address the psychosocial needs of those military families that live in the community. Even though their attendance often leads to better facilities, higher teacher pay, and more money for extracurricular activities, the particular needs of military children—ease of records transfers, facilitation of smooth progress through varying curricular requirements, active programs to encourage acceptance and integration of military children into the civilian environment, accommodations for children who are suffering the stress of parental deployment, to name a few—often go unaddressed.

Although the immediate and most obvious effects are often concerning, when one looks closely at the long-lasting psychological and psychosocial effects, the picture is even bleaker. In her 1991 landmark study, *Military Brats: Legacies of Childhood Inside the Fortress*, Mary Edwards Wertsch, a Military Brat herself, argues that "not only does the military constitute a separate and distinctly different subculture from civilian America, it exercises such a powerful shaping influence on its children that for the rest of our lives we continue to bear its stamp" (xii–xiii). In other words, one never really stops being a Military Brat, as our adult lives are shaped by that stamp. Military Brats grow to adulthood carrying the legacies of life in what she calls "the Fortress." Wertsch continues, noting that this "warrior society" is marked by "a rigid authoritarian structure ... extreme mobility; a great deal of father absence; isolation and alienation from the civilian community; an exceedingly strict class system; a very high incidence of alcoholism ... a deeply felt sense of mission; and, not least, an atmosphere of constant preparation for war, with the accompanying

# Introduction

implication for every family that on a moment's notice the father can be sent to war, perhaps never to be seen again" (xiii). Authoritarian parenting, extreme mobility, a strict class system, constant preparation for war, and potential loss of primary or secondary parents shape the lives and the psyches of these children in ways that those children, and the larger culture that they eventually enter as adults, have not fully grasped. Adding to this is the very real sense that Military Brats have that they are a "bothersome necessity" to the overall mission, as Wertsch puts it, "like the camp followers of whom they formed a not coincidental part" (xv). Unfortunately, little has changed for military children in the decades that have followed Wertsch's book, and Brats today still find themselves extraneous to both the civilian and military worlds.

As novelist Pat Conroy, perhaps one of the best-known Military Brats, whose works will be discussed in later chapters, says, Military Brats are a "tribe" and "an undiscovered nation" with few signs visible to the outside world (xvii). However, the effects of life inside the Fortress linger and spread outward into the lives of those with whom they intersect and create. As Wertsch says, the "notion that we children of the Fortress were raised in ways substantially different from our civilian peers is a realization that hovers on the edge of consciousness in childhood. The truth of it is undeniable, but we focus on it at our own peril. It is safer to take note of it later, when we are older and have some power over our lives" (10).

While Brats recognize, at some level, that their lives are very different from those of their civilian counterparts, they also suspect that looking too closely at the structures that underlie their upbringing can be dangerous, both for their own mental health and for the larger mission to which their parents have dedicated their lives in the most literal sense. Paying close attention to the unreasonable demands placed on military children can lead to despair or anger, even as it can sometimes result in understanding and insight. Perhaps Brats cannot examine the world too closely while they are in it, but scrutiny after the fact—in the form of works that will be discussed here—can be therapeutic.

A more expansive way to think of Brat life, according to Wertsch,

*Introduction*

is "like being drafted into a gigantic theater company" (1), although one producing the mechanisms of destruction rather than entertainment. She adds that required behaviors on a military base "can have a staged, rehearsed feeling to them that is largely alien to the civilian world" (2). Military children grow up shopping at taxpayer-subsidized food stores, saluting the flag at designated times, falling asleep to "Taps" played on a loudspeaker, seeing men and women all around them saluting, marching, following orders and protocol, driving tanks, flying planes, leaving on ships and submarines, and returning home. Flags and music, costumes and backdrops, are all part of the military base experience.

However, Wertsch says, this is a drama company "with a difference. For these actors, there is no end to the production, no moment when they can leave the role behind. A warrior must be a warrior twenty-four hours a day; the script calls for him to be ready for war at any moment. The identification of the warrior-actors with their roles is total. For them, the boundary between what is real and what is not has long since ceased to matter" (11). In other words, in this drama the swords are real, and the deaths are not staged. Brats are simply extras in this drama, ones who are never asked to participate, except by saluting the flag, standing for the National Anthem at the base or post theater, and never, ever drawing attention away from the lead actors.

For the military parent, this drama involves wearing a mask that cannot be removed, one whose "function is to suppress the individual beneath it" (Wertsch 14). Masks, in the form of regulation haircuts, uniforms, and rules of conduct, are donned at boot camp or upon enrollment in one of the military academies, and they are masks "of the warrior: macho, aggressive, single-minded, able to respond instantly to any command, willing to lay down his life for his comrades" (14).

However, it is more than wearing a mask: it is "the decision to merge one's identity with the mask of the warrior" (Wertsch 17). It is also acceptance into the family that is the military, a family with very clear expectations and numerous rules. This can be "very reassuring, it its way. It offers security, identity, a sense of purpose" (17). For the warrior, much of this role can be very satisfying, although the costs to his

## Introduction

or her mental health and to the people in his or her care can be very high, and often not realized until many years later.

The effect on the children of warriors of living inside this strange and lethal theater is complex, and the message they receive is two-fold and contradictory. The first is *"This is a society prepared to wage war with the same relentless attention to detail it brings to every moment of every day"* (Wertsch 33, italics in the original), and the second is *"Don't even try to look beyond the surface. What you see is all you are authorized to see. The rest is off limits, classified, denied"* (34). Military Brats, then, are asked to be constantly aware of the mission, which is to defend the peace through acts of war, and, at the same time, not to inquire too closely into the relationship of their family to that well-oiled machine. For Brats to understand the world from which they came, they "must deliberately violate the cardinal rule of the society that gave us birth and trained us in its ways. Our task must be to get past the surface, search behind the masks, venture into the forbidden regions of interior life, claim for ourselves the hidden realm of feelings" (35). They must lift the masks and, in many cases, begin to direct their own lives, especially when they find themselves kicked out of the theater troupe at age 18. This is necessary if former Brats are ever to make lasting friendships and intimate connections with others.

There are several ways to do this necessary work: therapy, conversations and connections with fellow Brats, writing down one's life story, and reading the experiences—both factual and fictionalized—of those who have experienced life inside the Fortress. Perhaps these investigations into the stories of warriors and their children can help to defuse the myth of the Fortress, inside which, as Wertsch says, "what is sacred is not individual rights ... but the myth of a completely controlled, conformist society composed of individuals of unblemished character who strive at all times for perfection in their public service and in their private lives." Warriors, spouses, children—all are in service to the myth, which is the essential undergirding to the military concept of "readiness." For them, the masks of secrecy, stoicism, and denial are standard issue—the basic equipment without which the mission cannot be accomplished (37). Novels, biographies, and

## *Introduction*

autobiographies such as the ones discussed in this book refute this powerful myth by looking out from behind the curtain and resisting the "secrecy, stoicism, and denial" upon which this myth depends.

Such a personal investigation would penetrate the illusion, born from the pretense, despite all evidence to the contrary, "that what they are doing is just a job, an impersonal assignment, unremarkable in every way" (Wertsch 44). The costs of casting off this illusion can be high. Thus, an attention to the words of those who have experienced this life can help Brats interrogate this theatrical society, which is "particularly well equipped to conceal its most intensely destructive personal minidramas behind an immaculate façade of smoothly untroubled conventionality" (49). However, looking closely at the Fortress reveals one of the most demoralizing aspects of Brat life, which is that the mission comes first, the warrior second, and the spouse and brats are always last (61).

These Navy, Army, Marine, and Air Force Brats live surrounded by the instruments of war, see their fathers more often in uniform than in civilian clothes, are trained not to remark on (or to even notice) the endless preparations for war going on all around them, and are taught from birth to subordinate their own desires (for a consistent home, for parents who are present, for a respite from fear) to the larger mission. The experiences of these children and young adults need to be recorded for, shared with, and examined by others, both inside and outside of the military community. Only then will it be possible for Brats to feel that they have finally been seen and perhaps understood, and for the civilian community to recognize the debt they owe to these junior warriors.

It is the goal of this book to focus on the experiences of these Military Brats: to listen to their voices and to read the stories of their lives written by others, to see the ways in which they create imaginative worlds that reflect the Brat experience, and to help them to work through the fears and frustrations of military life. In searching for common themes and patterns in these stories, it may be possible to generalize about the Brat experience and, perhaps, to suggest possibilities for how children in the Fortress might be better served by the country to which they have been forced to dedicate their young lives.

# Introduction

To amplify the voices of Military Brats, this book will explore full-length biographies of former children of military parents in the first chapter. This chapter will explore theories about the reliability, methods, and issues of concern in autobiography, using critical material from Erich Goode's *Justifiable Conduct*, Kate Douglas' *Contesting Childhood*, Leigh Gilmore's *The Limits of Autobiography*, and Julia Watson and Sidonie Smith's *Women, Autobiography, Theory*. Then, the chapter will shift to Brat narratives, which include Les Arbuckle's *Saigon Kids*, William Willis's *Base Jumping*, G.E. Allingham's *Growing Up in Khaki*, Pat Conroy's *The Death of Santini*, Sharlene Stringer's *Speak Through Me*, Christine Kriha Kastner's *Soldiering on—Finding My Homes*, L. Diane Ryan's *Child of the Blue*, Gail Hosking Gilberg's *Snake's Daughter*, and Kim Medders' *The Italian Lesson*. These books tell stories that run the gamut from surprising to mundane and from hilarious to terrifying, often in the same narrative. They sing the praises of Military Brats—their resilience, creativity, and dedication to their country—while at the same time showing the dangers to which military life exposes them, both within and outside of their all-too-transient homes.

Chapter Two will continue to explore personal narratives by looking at collections of short, first-person stories of Brat life, including Mark Curtis et al.'s *Growing up Military*, Deborah Ellis' *Off to War*, and Mary R. Truscott's *Brats*. This chapter will consider all the issues raised in the previous chapter while noting the ways in which an editor might shape or alter these narratives. These collections also have the advantage of offering a variety of perspectives on the Brat experience rather than a single-voiced narrative from one perspective.

The third chapter will explore young adult novels such as Daphne Benedis-Grab's *Army Brats*, Vicki Bohe-Thackwell's *Too Skinny to Float*, Sarah Lewis Holmes' *Operation Yes*, Michael Joseph Lyons' *BRAT and the Kids of Warriors*, Ashlee Cowles' *Beneath Wandering Stars*, Rosanne Parry's *Heart of a Shepherd*, and Frances O'Roark Dowell's *Shooting the Moon*. These novels range in popularity and quality, but they all intend to send the message that Brat life can be exciting and sometimes even comical, while at the same time recognizing the dangers of living in a family dedicated to protecting the nation's

*Introduction*

peace. Despite the usually cheery tone of these novels, it is possible to glimpse in them some of the darker sides of Brat life explored in Wertsch's book. Young adult fiction also has the advantage of being accessible to younger Brats, who may find comfort in seeing themselves empathetically represented.

Novels intended for adults will be the focus of Chapter Four. This chapter will examine Pat Conroy's *The Great Santini*, Bobbie Ann Mason's *In Country*, Sarah Bird's *The Yokota Officers Club*, and Elizabeth Berg's *Durable Goods, Joy School,* and *True to Form*, from her Katie Nash series. These novels are far more harrowing than the young adult novels discussed in the previous chapter, but they also contain moments of adventure, humor, and pathos. Unlike works directed at children and young adults, these novels directly address physical and verbal abuse, alcoholism, the emotional toll of parental absence and/or death, and the gritty resolve of Brats in the face of these hardships.

Chapter Five will explore the lives of four famous Military Brats: science fiction writer and Scientology founder L. Ron Hubbard (Navy), The Doors lead singer Jim Morrison (Navy), politician and writer Newt Gingrich (Army), and YA novelist Suzanne Collins (Air Force). The goal of this chapter is to make connections between the attachment style generated in military families and the lives and creative choices of these four people. Although quite diverse in their personalities and impacts on their communities, these four people demonstrate similar patterns in their upbringings, attitudes about their parents and about life, and later adult behaviors.

The conclusion will look to the future—at what has been done in recent years (and what remains to be done) to mitigate the stress of Brat life, both inside and outside of the military. It will also consider what should be done in the future to help ensure that the children of America's warriors have, as much as possible, a carefree and "normal" childhood. It will also suggest ways in which those who have been Military Brats can learn to process these experiences in their adult lives. Ultimately, my hope is also that this book will give voice to the experiences, the sorrows, the fears, and the joys that Military Brats have had—and continue to have—and to help make the far-flung tribe of adult Brats feel less alone.

## Introduction

The aims of this book are both personal and political: I hoped in reading these autobiographies and novels to better understand the world from which I arose, and I hope that reading about these experiences will help other Brats, both current and former, to feel more connected to their Brat peers and to understand that while their lives are not "normal," they are familiar to anyone growing up in the Fortress.

I also hope that parents and teachers of Brats will become more aware of the specialized needs of this population, the sons and daughters of warriors. In addition, I hope that this book will reach the wider communities across the country that serve the military and its children. It is not enough to say "thank you for your service" to the occasional person we encounter in uniform. We owe these children, who never asked to serve their country but who serve it nevertheless, our attention and our support. We can—and should—do better.

# ONE

## "I rarely give up my vigilance, and I have no idea what it is I am waiting for"
### *Book-Length Autobiographies*

> I believe that we should *care* about how soldiers are trained, equipped, led, and welcomed home when they return from war. This is our moral duty toward those we ask to serve on our behalf, and it is in our own self-interest as well. Unhealed combat trauma blights not only the life of the veteran but the life of the family and community
> —Jonathan Shay, *Achilles in Vietnam*, 195

If "unhealed combat trauma" affects the veteran, his/her family, and the wider communities in which he or she lives—and the evidence clearly shows that it does—then studying the lives of those who have experienced combat and the families that wait for them to return can help us to understand and perhaps heal some of that trauma. To do this well, one needs to study both these life stories and the ways in which the writers choose to tell them. Since this book focuses on the experiences of Military Brats more directly than the experiences of adult veterans, this chapter will look at Brat autobiographies for the ways in which life in the Fortress has affected them. It will also look closely at how these Brats form their life narratives—what they choose to tell and what they choose to omit.

Theorizing about autobiographical writing has increased

dramatically in the last few decades, and this research has productively complicated the ways in which readers read and critics analyze personal narratives. At the most basic level, as Erich Goode points out in his 2013 book *Justifiable Conduct: Self-Vindication in Memoir*, "Authors keep audiences or significant others in mind when narrating their life stories; they anticipate criticisms from these relevant audiences as they unfold the details of their lives" (xi). In other words, autobiographical writers think about those who would be affected by what they write about their lives and the lives of their friends and family. Thinking about the potentially negative consequences of their work, writers may well soften or frame their narratives in ways that may cause the least disturbance—both for themselves and for the people in their lives.

This passage from Goode refers to stories that might be embarrassing to the writer or others in his or her life, stories which may not necessarily be traumatic ones. With trauma narratives, Leigh Gilmore says, "conventions about truth telling ... can be inimical to the ways in which some writers bring trauma stories into language. The portals are too narrow and the demands too restrictive" (*Limits* 3). It is difficult to tell such stories, according to Gilmore, because of both internal and external forces that limit what and (and what *should*) be told. Gilmore adds that "the judgments [autobiographical narratives] invite may be too similar to forms in which trauma was experienced. When the contest is over who can tell the truth, the risk of being accused of lying (or malingering, or inflating, or whining) threatens the writer into continued silence" (3). When faced with the choice of telling one's truth and thereby suffering the trauma of not being believed, or having one's trauma minimized, a writer may choose silence over this new kind of pain. Gilmore reiterates, "Although those who can tell their stories benefit from the therapeutic balm of words, the path to this achievement is strewn with obstacles" (7). Writers of trauma narratives may thus find themselves retraumatized by readers who mistrust both the form in which the writer chooses to tell the story and, at times, even the authenticity of the narrative. Telling one's life story inevitably means telling the stories of others and thereby being exposed to their pain and anger, as well as their disbelief.

## One. "I rarely give up my vigilance"

Perhaps most significant for narratives about lives of children in the military, "the cultural work performed in the name of autobiography profoundly concerns representations of citizenship and the nation" (Gilmore 12). If autobiography has the potential to raise questions in readers' minds about the state, then a trauma narrative about life as a Military Brat challenges not only military structures/support systems but also the nation(s) that created those structures. Autobiography also contradicts to the message that Brats receive from early childhood: tell no one what goes on here. Brats are, after all, trained from birth to represent positively—through their actions and their words—for their military parent(s), the military in general, and the United States. Telling harrowing stories from their childhoods means Military Brats are violating that training and could bring shame not just to the writer, but also to his or her family, and even to the nation. This magnifies the trauma by extending it to a national scale: disclosures, especially those about current situations in the military, could damage soldiers' ability of fight (and to survive). Therefore, it is no wonder that so few Brats have told their stories. Loose lips sink ships, after all.

This culture of denial and secrecy exacerbates a problem that exists with much autobiographical writing: the unreliability of memory, especially when one is recounting childhood experiences. In *Contesting Childhood*, Kate Douglas says that "for an adult writing an autobiography of childhood, childhood memories are at best fragile and fragmented and at worse impossible to retrieve" (21). Fragmented, fragile, and, perhaps, forever lost, stories from childhood can be frustratingly difficult to recall accurately. Autobiographies, she continues, "are laden with memory loss, memory gaps, false memory, and a plethora of other memory-related controversies" (21). Adults trying to recall and subsequently tell their childhood experiences thus face a host of obstacles, not least of which is that memory is notoriously unreliable.

In short, Douglas says, writing one's autobiography is complicated: "We are intrinsically aware of what we are supposed to remember and document, of which stories and events are culturally valuable, of what is speakable and unspeakable (at any given time) about our childhoods" (23). Childhood memories are, therefore, inflected by the various scripts people write in their heads, scripts based on cultural expectations about childhood and available *aides-mémoire*. Adding to these "culturally valuable" models for the Military Brat is the Brat as resilient, resourceful, and, finally, committed to the family's purpose. Defeating this sense of disloyalty to country (as well as to family) can be an almost-insurmountable obstacle to the writing of the Brat autobiography.

One response to challenges like these is to take refuge in nostalgia, according to Douglas: "Nostalgic autobiographies of childhood have an enduring cultural fascination.... For those engaged in writing and reading autobiographies of childhood, the child often functions as a symbol of the past, a cultural mechanism for reconstructing, and to some extent mourning, the distant past" (86). For the Military Brat, this could involve the re-creation of a time (often imaginary) in which the military was respected by the nation as a whole and when the father's word was law. Another common nostalgic response, especially in the autobiographies of Military Brats, is to emphasize the autobiographer's sense of humor and general pluckiness. As Douglas says, "Anger and regret are not valuable commodities in autobiographical writing about childhood. Humor and resilience amid trauma are" (137). Not surprisingly, then, several of the autobiographies in this chapter will stress both this humor in the face of family violence and international turmoil and resilience in the face of traumatic events such as verbal and physical abuse, regime change, war, and death.

Finally, Douglas says, "To read a (well-chosen) autobiography of childhood is to have selected a text that has sociological value beyond the individual. The resilient survivor-author has offered his or her text to the reader as a testimony and has asked the reader to witness this testimony though the act of reading" (168). Thus, autobiographies can become cultural touchstones, models that other writers can follow and experiences from which readers may learn. In the case of Military Brat autobiographies, this could consist of showing the ways in which the dislocations and isolation of military families are sources of adventure and bonding or explain how the family violence simmering under the surface of many military families is justified by the stress of the mission. However, it could also mean raising the curtain on the theatricality of military life and showing how the costumes are old and threadbare, the sets are creaky and in danger of collapsing, and the actors themselves are not always convinced of the rightness of their roles.

These conflicting modes of representation can be seen in Kelsey Schertz and Cassidy Watson's short essay in *The Journal of Public Health*, "What Becomes of America's Military Brats?" Undergraduates at the University of Minnesota School of Public Health and Military Brats themselves, Schertz and Watson say that the term "Military Brats" is "a label that transcends race, religion, age, military branch, and parental rank, one that silos military children into their own subculture marked by hardship and patriotism" (837). Note the juxtaposition of "hardship and patriotism," which casts the struggles of Military Brats to belong, to feel rooted, as one that is superseded by their love of country. While admitting that "growing up in the military is both physically and mentally disruptive" and admitting that after multiple deployments resilience can "wear thin," Schertz and Watson say there is a pride in saying that "once you are a military brat, you are always a military brat" (837). The loss of loved ones and the stress of frequent moves is here obscured by a sense of belonging to a group of fellow survivors. This cognitive dissonance—my childhood was difficult but it is all for the best—would likely not be sustainable in an essay longer than a single page.

Indeed, Schertz and Watson acknowledge that there is very little research into what happens to Military Brats after they age out of their military childhoods. Lack of records on former military children and the reflexive secrecy of the military surrounding all aspects of personnel matters have exacerbated this problem. Nevertheless, Schertz and Watson say that we should keep in mind that military children do grow up and "carry experiences that warrant attention" (837). One hopes that, given their training in public health, this new breed of researchers with experience of Brat life will begin to explore this group of voiceless people.

Until such research is available, however, personal memoirs of the Brat experience will have to suffice. Some are stories of traditional

## Brat Life

Brat life; others are more exotic; still others are the stories of the effects that wartime trauma had on the families at home. Recounting childhoods from the 1940s to the 1980s, Les Arbuckle's *Saigon Kids*, Sandy Hanna's *The Ignorance of Bliss*, Gail Hosking Gilberg's *Snake's Daughter*, Ben and Anne Purcell's *Love and Duty*, Louise Steinman's *The Souvenir*, Diane Ryan's *Child of the Blue*, and, finally, Pat Conroy's *The Death of Santini* all explore the unusual challenges and the peculiar pleasures of life as a military child. While they often participate in the nostalgia and self-censorship described above, taken as whole, this collection of stories comes close to describing the complexities and the conflicts of the lives of Military Brats.

Some of the more interesting autobiographies, especially to anyone with experience/memories of the Vietnam War period, focus on dependents who were stationed with their fathers in Vietnam before official U.S. involvement in the war. These stories are unfamiliar to most people, even to those of us who grew up alongside the military engagement in Vietnam. A good example is Les Arbuckle's 2017 *Saigon Kids: An American Military Brat Comes of Age in 1960s Vietnam*, which tells a story of his time as a Military Brat in Vietnam that is equal parts harrowing and hilarious. Arbuckle's father managed Armed Forces Radio in Saigon from 1962 to 1964, when the U.S. was just beginning its involvement with Vietnam. Les, two of his brothers, and his mother joined his father, known as "Doc," there and lived "on the economy," as military and diplomatic families refer to living outside of military bases in foreign countries.

Les, who was 13 when they arrived, had a life that included daredevil rides on unregulated go-carts, sex with Vietnamese prostitutes, and encounters with a pedophilic soldier who provided Les and his friends with cigarettes in exchange for oral sex. He also recounts making homemade rockets, fighting with local teenaged gangsters; roaming the streets at all hours; seeing and hearing tanks, gunfire, and Buddhist monks immolating themselves; and hiding under the dining room table to avoid artillery during various political uprisings. In addition to these dramatic and often shocking events, Les also recounts the more normal aspects of young adulthood: dating, going to dances, taking rides on motorbikes, sneaking beers, harassing substitute teachers,

## One. "I rarely give up my vigilance"

participating in food fights in the cafeteria. Despite nearly being killed several times, he describes Saigon as "the best place I'd ever lived" (17). With its bravado and optimism, this autobiography clearly demonstrates the challenges of self-writing for the Military Brat.

Despite his sometimes rosy and occasionally curiously affectless recollections of his time in Vietnam, Arbuckle's discussion of the family's deployment to Saigon has all the negative hallmarks of the Military Brat experience. Although the family did not want to move to Vietnam, "a military family isn't a democracy. Military transfers are commands, not suggestions or requests" (19). "Commands, not suggestions" determine when and where (not *if*) the family will move, and military children have no say in the matter. At this juncture, Les decides that he "wasn't cut out to be a military Brat, because the thought of leaving Florida filled me with despair" (24). Nevertheless, they do leave, and Les says he remains "haunted by the prospect of a desolate future without friends or a real home. I couldn't shed the feeling that I was missing something; that the parade of life was about the pass me by as I watched from the sidelines" (27). It is interesting that Arbuckle chooses military metaphors to describe the alienating experience of moving so often. He is standing on the sidelines (as military children do at parades) watching the parade pass him by. One assumes that this feeling of desolation, of bystander status, continues throughout Arbuckle's life, as it does in the lives of many Brats.

Les's life as a Brat consisted of "arrive, make friends ('acquaintances' would be more accurate), then leave, never to see any of them again" (28). Frequent moves make it difficult, if not impossible, to make lifelong friendships. He especially remembers leaving his dog behind (not the first time he had to face this sad reality): "The scene was always the same: four boys gathered around their dog (who had no idea what was going on), each boy sniffing back tears as he gave her one last hug. Like death-row lawyers, we always turned our sad faces to Mother and Doc, praying for a last-minute reprieve, but it never came" (62–63). Note the language here: the boys are "sniffing back tears" and feeling like "death-row lawyers." Often, a pet is the only constant in a military child's life outside of his immediate family, and to be forced to abandon it (not once but several times over the course of a childhood) can be traumatic and reinforces the transitoriness of military life and, perhaps, the powerlessness of the Brats within it.

After they have said goodbye to friends and pets, shipped out, and arrived in Saigon, things were not peaceful in their new home in Vietnam, where his parents' "preferred anxiety-relieving medicine was generous quantities of booze" (31) and where his father's unpredictable anger made Les hope that he would not be its target (this time) (44).

Not surprisingly, the problems, both inside and outside of the home, continue for Les throughout his stay in Saigon. Although he felt more comfortable in the American Community School he attended in Vietnam than in civilian schools in the States, he still felt like "an outsider among outsiders, a stranger among strangers" (84). Living off base also had its frustrations, as they were staying outside of the "protective bubble" of an American military installation (96). This is a burden particular to children who have followed their parents overseas: they feel at home only in protected compounds like diplomatic missions or military bases, but these places can also monitor and restrict their behaviors.

There were also the added dangers of embarrassing one's father and running the risk of damaging his military career. After he and a friend were filmed watching a Buddhist protest, for example, Les's father is furious because his commanding officer finds out: "I knew that enlisted personnel had sometimes been transferred because of the misdeeds of their Brats. 'You have to be careful around here, [his mother says] because everybody sees what you do, being American and all'" (148). The culture of surveillance Wertsch describes exists not just on the military base: it can be equally oppressive off base, especially when one is living in a war-torn and potentially dangerous area like Vietnam in the 1960s. The reasoning goes that the father who cannot control his wayward family (whether wife or children) cannot be trusted to lead his men into battle. An orderly family leads to an orderly mission.

Despite all the drama and struggle Les experiences in Vietnam, he feels an attachment to the place, which is common in Brat life. As Les watches some of his classmates leave for the States, he realizes "Saigon was a home to which they could never return" (149). This is certainly

## One. "I rarely give up my vigilance"

true, given what was about to happen in Vietnam after 1965, when Military Brats would no longer be running amok on Saigon's streets. Despite the dangers, though, Les never worried about "living in a place as volatile as Saigon.... Terrorist attacks and riots had become commonplace, but I still wanted to be with my friends, not exiled to some crushingly boring suburb in America. The burdens of finding new friends, starting at a new school, and learning the ins and outs of a new neighborhood seemed more daunting as I grew older" (292). After the excitement, danger, and relative freedom of life in Vietnam, Les finds America "crushingly boring." This is a familiar Brat experience: one prefers living with a certain amount of danger, as opposed to being surrounded with civilians who, in their secure and stable lives, could never understand the life into which you have been conscripted.

Eventually, the difficulties of life in increasingly dangerous Vietnam takes their toll on his father, who, in a manner that Pat Conroy has made famous in his books, takes his frustrations out on Les. After Les comes home drunk one evening, his father, who is likely as drunk as his son, "cupped his right hand and swung hard. He caught me on the ear, knocking me onto the toilet. As I rose, dizzy from the slap, he strained to elbow Mother aside. His eyes were flashing with an anger that I'd never seen before. This wasn't going to be the same kind of thrashing he dished out when he was upset at my brothers and me" (244). His mother stops that fight, but Les says that he cannot "imagine a world where Doc and I were not at odds with each other, a state of affairs that had been in effect as long as I could remember" (246).

The familiar lesson is reinforced here: if Les chooses to express his personal desires or adolescent rebellion in any way, he will be at odds with his father. His father's world "was organized around the rules and regulations of the military—a strict, no-nonsense society of discipline that demanded and received loyalty and obedience without question, but I hadn't sworn an oath to a set of government regulations. I remained a sensitive and self-absorbed youth, reckless and moody, dismissive of adult authority and hell-bent on discovering for myself what made the world spin" (306). Like other Brats discussed in this study, especially young men, "loyalty and obedience without question" becomes increasingly difficult to square with a "reckless and moody" adolescence. One could easily be talking about Jim Morrison here, as well Pat Conroy, and numerous other male Brats.

Sadly, although he sought his father's approval and attention, like many of the other male Brats in this sturdy, Les rarely received either, "so ambivalence might be a better word [than hate] to describe the way I felt toward him, even as he lay dying" (308). Fathers and sons (especially angry fathers and rebellious sons) often clash, but this is a father who has taken an oath to do what he is told, regardless of the consequences, in conflict with a son who is expected to live by similar rules, ones to which he has never sworn allegiance. Like Pat Conroy and Jim Morrison, Les realizes the difficulties of having a father who has dedicated his life to following orders and who therefore has little time for his family, which can create irresolvable fissures in family life.

Despite all this conflict, on the plane back to the U.S., Les realizes how lucky he was to live there: "Violence, poverty, war, disease, and the adventure of living amongst the gentle, good-natured South Vietnamese people had spared me the stultifying boredom of the middle-class suburban life I'd lived in the States. But I'd also gained friends who shared the wonders of this unusual life, and within our group, a strong bond had formed" (301). As is common in Brat narratives, the various traumas caused by frequent moves, life in foreign countries, and hidden family violence are subsumed by the "strong bond" between Brats with similar experiences.

However, the Brats, unlike their fathers and the other soldiers, "had no patches to wear on our shoulders, no ribbons for our chests. We would receive no proud salutes or award ceremonies for our service. Our stories would not be published, our tales would remain untold; there would be no commendations, movies, or other recognition of our unique yet unforgettable place in history" (303). They have no outward signs of their service to their country and, until recently, their "tales would remain untold." Brats may feel emotionally connected to each other, but, realistically, as they will likely never be stationed in the same place together again and face challenges finding each other again, that bond becomes largely illusory.

These early life experiences leave a legacy of feeling different and bereft: "I am often beset by a feeling of isolation that lingers deep

## One. "I rarely give up my vigilance"

within me, a cloud that will, without warning or provocation, intrude on the sunniest of my days," Les comments. "It's not a feeling of loneliness, but *aloneness,* of being apart from the mainstream of America's people. No matter where I live, I feel as though I'm standing on the outer edge of the community, never quite knowing what it's like to be on the inside" (303). He says he shares a feeling with other Brats, "the fear of being forgotten" (304). This is an interesting way of phrasing it, feeling alone but not lonely. Brats learn quickly to bury feelings like loneliness, as they cause them to regret or resent circumstances over which they have no control. Still, they recognize that their lives have in some ways rendered them unable to connect to those who have never moved, never seen the world, or never sacrificed anything for their country. In many ways, Les (like many other Brats) has never left Vietnam or the military, even though he has been living a civilian life his entire adulthood. He stands on the outside of the larger community, worried that his childhood sacrifice will be forgotten. By telling his harrowing story, he is finding a way to be remembered.

Sandy Hanna's 2019 *The Ignorance of Bliss: An American Kid in Saigon* is another story of American children posted to Vietnam with their families. Her father was a colonel, and they were in Vietnam from 1960 to 1962, when the military were officially designated "observers." This was part of my own experience as well, although my Army-officer father spent 1963 in Saigon without his family. As with most Military Brats, Hannah details both the positive and negative aspects of life as a Brat. Military children's experiences, she says, are "ever-changing," allowing them to "travel to foreign lands and experience things that most can't even imagine" (1). Thus, she starts her story with the positive, as is common in many of these narratives. Military life may be changeable, and sometimes difficult, she cheerfully states, but it offers opportunities for travel that most children never experience.

However, it is also a life that takes danger for granted, as when the kids slip past armed South Vietnamese soldiers to go on a dangerous adventure (18). Undeterred by the weapons, which were "a familiar sight for military kids," they took risks most civilian children could only dream about (18). These risks were always taken without their parents finding out, and silence became "standard operating procedure" for the siblings (23). The price one pays for such "risks" and the excitement accompanying them wis silence in front of one's parents. The "standard operating procedure" for Military Brats always involves deception and secrecy, far more so than for civilian children, for whom national (and in this case international) security is not a concern.

As with Les Arbuckle's memoir, Hanna's narrative also shows the ways that Military Brats learn early to subsume their desires underneath the larger mission when they were required to move. If they complained, they "were told we represented America—so shape up and fly right!" (27). Like soldiers themselves, Brats were admonished to follow orders uncomplainingly. Hanna, like many other Brat autobiographers, turns this early programming into a positive character trait. The best way to describe Brats, she says, is "adaptive" and "a tribe unto ourselves": "We pick up languages and accents quickly. Material things just aren't important to us. We leave them behind us as we do our lives, our friends, our pets, and our teachers. Nomadic and in some cases feral, we bond immediately with kids who are like us, displaced and transient" (28). The language here is interesting. Brats are "feral," reacting with hostility to "strange creatures" in the civilian world, while at the same time adopting the protective coloration of accents and languages. This may present as adaptability, but, as in nature, it is merely the way one survives. Blend in, do not make waves, fly right, and leave pets and friends and houses behind without a backward glance. This is a roadmap for emotional detachment, not necessarily an indicator of "grit."

Hanna explains this further. In general, she says, "Military kids take control in order to feel their world is not out of control. Imagine moving every two years and never having any idea where you are going next. Orders came in, and usually there was no time to say goodbyes to any attachments you might have made" (212). Leaving one's current home "never seemed to cause any of us issues. There was never an expectation of seeing anyone we knew again anyway. It would be unusual if we did. BRATs are used to it. To make a big deal about this would have been much ado about nothing" (313). While Hanna attempts to get nonmilitary folks to understand what life for the Brat

***One. "I rarely give up my vigilance"***

is like, she also insists that these traumatic dislocations "never seemed to cause any of us issues." One imagines that someone outside military culture would find that a rather strange and possibly unreflective statement. However, the Military Brat learns quickly that there is no point making "much ado about nothing." The nothing, though, is the child's desire to feel grounded, rooted, and in some control over his or her life, something one ought to make a fuss about losing.

Although Hanna insists that Brats are taught not to show vulnerability and to adapt to the world around them, their experiences in Vietnam left each of the children with baggage they did not know they were carrying, which would "come at us like a freight train in the middle of the night" (64). In addition, as other female Brats, including Wertsch, have reported, being a girl in a resolutely masculine world can be difficult. Her entire life, the author "always felt vulnerable on Army posts. These were places made up of enlisted men, officers, and adolescents mimicking their male-dominated society" (83). A world in which the masculine virtues of strength, power, and toughness are prized is not one that is very safe for girls. In addition, although her father was harder on the boys "to make them capable of taking care of themselves in the world," he didn't "apply the same standards to the girls. He expected less of them" (127). These are the twin legacies of Brat life for girls: life in a vaguely menacing environment combined with a sense that no one who matters takes one's dreams for the future seriously.

As is also typical in Brat stories, the father's unpredictable anger is a predictable part of the children's lives. After their father beats her brother with a strap for swearing, Hanna comments that "the Colonel's actions were baffling to us kids and his anger seemed misplaced" (126). Notice that she calls him "the Colonel" here as a way of distancing her father from the actions he takes. In behaving as "the Colonel," he is released from his obligations to be a kind and compassionate father, and he must enforce the rules of military decorum. The kids "find themselves" in this situation, a weirdly passive way of describing what happened. Also, she comments right after this that the "beautiful sunny day" simply turned "ugly," not that her father's ugly behavior marked the day—and their lives—forever. This fear of unpredictable violence overshadows the childhoods of many Brats, early years in which relatively minor infractions often result in physical or verbal attacks. To make matters worse, her brother blamed her for the attack, which she had provoked by encouraging her younger brother to swear.

After that point, Hanna says, her brother "looked at me with a deep distrust that never would be repaired in our lifetime. The Colonel never accepted his responsibility and continued to remain a mystery to me" (126–7). This is true for many Brats: the unpredictable and violent father never apologizes, never explains, and never becomes a fully-fledged human being for his children (or perhaps even for himself). Committed to a cause beyond himself, the father as "Colonel" never questions his actions, just as he is bound not to question those in authority over him.

In Hanna's story, as in the stories of many of these children, Military Brats are told that everything they do—good or bad—reflects on their fathers. "There was no room for error, just obedience at all times" (239), a task that is, of course, impossible for children. They were also not supposed to show fear or disappointment: "As children of a military officer, we were told to grin and bear it, whatever it was. And that we did" (239). Ultimately, they were "good soldiers. We took it all on the chin, in true military fashion" (315). Fly right, take it on the chin, grin and bear it—these are useful strategies for going through boot camp but not necessarily the most productive skills when trying to grow into a happy adult. This denial of feelings can lead to depression and anxiety in later years as former Brats struggle to decipher just exactly what they might be feeling, given that they got so good at denying and burying their emotions as children.

The training in stoicism that Hanna and others describe in their memoirs does not serve them well in their adult lives. Life in the civilian world, Hanna says, "would prove to be an assignment more difficult for me than anything that had come before" (337). Without their immediate family around them, these children find it difficult to adapt (338). It appears that passive acceptance of any of life's blows and changes may not be the best preparation for life outside the Fortress. For those Brats who do not enlist or marry into the military, life in the

## One. "I rarely give up my vigilance"

civilian world can seem—and remain for decades—strange, uninviting, and hostile.

Although it is also a Vietnam story, Gail Hosking Gilberg's 1997 autobiography *Snake's Daughter: The Roads in and out of War* does not recount the author's experiences "In Country," as time in Vietnam was designated by those who served there. Instead, it tells the story of her father, an Army sergeant in the Special Forces, who was killed in 1967 during his third tour in Vietnam. Trying to understand the "curious hold" that Vietnam had on her father (5), Gilberg uses his photographs to help her understand his life behind what she saw as a "guarded gate." Behind that gate was a "world a daughter can't know intimately—men and the military" (10). Her challenge in writing this book was how to "enter the off-limits zone I learned not to violate as the daughter of a warrior" (58). For her as a female Brat, much of the world of the fathers, the world of the military (especially combat), was closed to her, as Wertsch discusses at length. She also attempts to puzzle out the conflicts between her father's love for the Army and the Special Forces and his love for his family: "He had quite separate roles, and it was often too difficult to play both at the same time" (81). The Special Forces soldier, who must keep his work secret from his family, is forced even more fully into such dual—and contradictory—roles.

In *The Military Family in Peace and War*, Thomas C. Mountz says this about Special Forces soldiers: "There is no task or mission that will not be attempted. When the risks are high and the stakes higher, the inner drive kicks in and makes the operator a precision machine.... The [Special Forces] operator exacts the same type of effort and commitment to the task from his fellow operator and also from his partner and family. It is not an expectation of perfection, just an expectation of maximum support with no hesitation" (122–23). The Special Forces soldier is resolute, unafraid, and almost automatic in his actions. Having a father who is a "precision machine," who is silent about the dangers he faces, can create a need to understand and empathize that may be partially fulfilled by such an autobiography. If she can attempt to tell his story, perhaps she will better understand her father. However, having a father who expects "maximum support with no hesitation" from his spouse and children may create an emotional landscape that is very difficult to change, regardless of how much time one spends recalling and recounting the past. Ultimately, such a father may be unknowable beyond his service to his country.

Gilberg's life as a Military Brat echoes the other accounts of the children of the military. She had an "unspoken sense" that everything was "ephemeral." Time is "fragmented," homes and families can be uprooted or even destroyed. "The thought of death lingers over any army camp," she comments (37). She spent much of her time tiptoeing around her father, "trying to sense his mood, trying to meet his expectations" (41) and attempting to look normal, which she calls "the mask an army base uses to survive" (43). In spite of this mask, though, she says, "What pumps through every military family's veins is a fear of which direction history will take and the question of where it will leave us in its squeeze" (44). Children of such parents learn to gauge the mood of adults and to respond accordingly; they are "parentified," as psychologists say, to an extreme degree. If they do not pay attention to the world around them—to things spoken and unspoken—it is quite possible that they may miss a final encounter with a military parent or do or say something that might result in endangering that parent.

As the daughter of a military father, Gilberg also faced problems particular to female children in the male-dominated world of the military, a world in which "only men can make a difference." She was "watching men control the lives of women, and feeling invisible when my father is away so much. I watched women afraid to live with men and afraid to live without them" (46). This is a kind of double invisibility: only men "make a difference" in this world, and children without a father (especially female children) often feel "invisible." Yet when the men *are* home, both their wives and their children often live in fear, which gives even more reason to try to remain unseen, unnoticed, unprotected.

She also describes the iconic moment on a military base when "retreat would blow, and all of us—soldiers and children alike—stopped whatever we were doing and stood in silence, hands over our hearts, while the American flag was lowered for the day" (62). This is a moment of shared patriotism, but it is also one fraught with worry: if one fails to honor the flag correctly, one risks public censure and private violence. Also, there is a superstitious element to it: if one fails in one's public and private duties to the country and to the military, not only could the service member be reprimanded—he might even die.

In addition, Gilberg describes the peculiar mix of public display and personal invisibility that permeates life for dependents on a military base: "The men saluted only each other and were aware of my presence only as a military dependent. They provided youth activities on base like bingo, swimming lessons, and camp, as if those would keep us out of the way.... 'Army dependent' said it all. They could function without us, but we couldn't without them" (158).

Brats find different ways of coping with these stressors. Gilberg took refuge in the permanence of her grandmother's home, which "created a stability my family lacked. In my many visits back to her home she taught me that history matters, that the details of one's home can make a difference in our lives" (67). At her grandmother's house, Gilberg finds both history and stability. There, she also engaged in her family's private and public denial that they were under stress. During the times her father was in Vietnam, Gilberg finds herself "teaching strangers how big my smile could be. I taught them that war didn't affect families and that daughters could be safe without fathers. I tried to teach my sisters that if we ignored the obvious empty chair at the table, by magic it wouldn't affect us" (96). Military Brats are always conscious of the impression they are making on their peers and even on their other family members. One must keep up the cheerful front or face acknowledging the errors of having one's father risking his life in a foreign country.

Later, Gilberg finds that during anti-war protests in college, she "often felt like a stranger among my peers, but neither would I have felt at home within the fortress. I had built a wall inside myself instead" (94). Not surprisingly, when one builds a wall against the reality of one's existence, that wall does not come down easily, if ever. From this passage, one can see that Wertsch does not call it a "Fortress" for nothing, and yet this passage reveals that the sturdiest walls might be the internal ones, not the guards, fences, and barriers surrounding the base.

## Brat Life

In spite of this internal wall, Gilberg feels a kinship with a crowd gathering to welcome soldiers home from the Iraq war, in spite of her friends' indignant criticisms of the military involvement in that conflict: "I knew, as army brats know, what that crowd knew—that all they truly wanted was to hold again that person who had left with rifle in hand for a foreign place, none of us knowing if he would ever return" (44). At that moment, political protests pale beside the need for families to be reunited. Despite her protests against the war, then, Gilberg's strongest emotional attachment is to other military families. She, unlike her college classmates, knows what it feels like to wait, anxiously, at home for a service member to return.

The repercussions of this wall-building, denial, and fear on Gilberg's adult life have been profound. She says, "I rarely give up my vigilance, and I have no idea what it is I am waiting for" (136). This hypervigilance has been recognized as the result of trauma, in this case the trauma of never knowing where one will be, whether one's family will remain intact. She also finds that giving personal items away "became a physical act of release. A feeling of safety would overcome me as I drove bags of things to the Goodwill. I believed that sheer owning could choke me of life, and I had to protect myself" (75). To divest is to remind oneself that possessions, like a permanent home or a father that was home most nights, are not a necessary part of her existence. She could live without them. Interestingly, though, giving away one's possessions can also be a sign of suicidal ideation.

Gilberg's relationship to her country becomes fraught as well: "I wasn't sure what being an American was. In an odd way I was purged of that place called America because I lived removed from its mass" (159). She also has trouble describing the life she led as a Brat: "I wanted to describe life in the fortress, but I never knew where to begin. I became a social chameleon instead" (162). Again, protective coloration becomes what saves the Brat from feeling ostracized or being victimized, but it also leads to a sense of impermanence and insincerity in personal relationships, as well as identity fragmentation.

Ultimately, though, Gilberg's view of the future is optimistic. She dreams of a time "when protestors could sit at the table with daughters of warriors and talk about their differences and recognize their

## One. "I rarely give up my vigilance"

similarities" (163). She also reminds her readers that "there are many voices in war" (173). There are the voices of the soldiers, of course, and of the military structures on both sides, the civilian casualties, the veterans, the children and spouses of the warriors, *and* the people who protest war. It is not clear whether her vision will come to pass, but memoirs like Gilberg's are a positive first step. Until the civilian world can see the life of a Military Brat, with all its joys and all its flaws, that healing conversation cannot begin.

Louise Steinman's 2001 autobiography *The Souvenir* does not recount Brat life in the ways the previous books have, but, like Gilberg, she chronicles her father's war experiences and the secrets he brought home with him. After her parents die, Steinman comes across a box of more than 500 letters her father Norman wrote to her mother while he was serving in the Pacific Theater in World War II. She also found a souvenir Japanese flag, which she eventually returned to the family of its original owner. To understand more about his experience and about him in general, she must piece together his experiences from the letters, as he never spoke about the war after he returned.

As is often the case for many Brats, their parents, who have served in war, are emotionally distant and prone to unpredictable rages. Steinman says about her father, "Emotional distress was not in his purview. His own, he kept private" (7). Her father "discussed neither his losses nor his sorrows" (7). This, too, is a common experience for children of veterans who have served during wartime. Steinman was also warned by her mother not to provoke her father's anger, which was "infrequent but explosive." When her father was angry or depressed, "a familiar and untouchable bad feeling permeated the house. Usually, he just smoldered, but on those occasions when he blew his top, the household froze in its tracks until he retired to his room and slammed the door with reverberating force" (8). These rages were explained away by Steinman's mother as tiredness from his job as a pharmacist and never linked to his time in the Pacific Theater. It became "standard family policy to spare my father exposure to unpredictable circumstances or raw emotion.... Better he be isolated than grapple with difficult feelings" (18–19). Steinman's story resembles those of many military children with violent and unpredictable fathers; the families of these men come to believe they must protect and shield as a way of preventing their outbursts. The results of this, though, are that the children of warriors never really get to know their fathers in their attempts to keep them from exploding, and the children grow up afraid and, eventually, numb.

When Steinman finally reads his letters, she finds that her father, in his letters, was very different from the angry and unpredictable person she had known. This creates mixed emotions in her: "My exhilaration at glimpsing my father's former self was tempered with sadness when I understood how the war had sealed off his emotions" (41). She comes to believe that her real father had been stolen from her before she was born (75). Again, the war—any war—steals a major part of the military father's emotional range and leaves him silent, withdrawn, and sometimes angry. This leaves the child confused, concerned, and feeling powerless to do anything about those feelings.

Steinman's trip to the Philippines and eventually to Japan to return the fraught "souvenir" taught her that children's lives "reverberate with the loss of their parents in ways their parents might never have imagined. They would become part of their dream life, their heritage—the way my father's experiences in the mountains of northern Luzon were part of mine, though he had never spoken of them" (76). The same is true for full-time Military Brats: the traumas that their fathers (and, more recently, their mothers) experienced during war are passed down to the families through violence, depression, isolation, and silence. These autobiographical accounts, like Steinman's *The Souvenir*, attempt to break that silence.

Different than the other stories written by adult children about their parents' experiences in the military, but resonant nonetheless, Ben and Anne Purcell's 1992 *Love and Duty* tells the story of Ben's experience from 1968 to 1973 as a prisoner of war in Vietnam. Much of the story is about Bill's harrowing experiences, but Anne also recounts the effects of his imprisonment on their children, which reveals connections to other Brat stories. One child, Cliff, who was seven at the time, has stomachaches that are thought to be related to his father's absence and his very real anxiety that he might not return. Anne decides not to let the children watch television, which was at that time bringing the war into America's living and dining rooms (34). This is also a common Brat experience, especially during the Vietnam War, when media coverage was often horrifying and critical of America's involvement. Children of soldiers who were or had been fighting in Vietnam often felt as if society was critiquing their fathers, and, by implication, them. This would leave them reluctant to listen to the news, read newspapers, or engage in conversations that might be perceived as disloyal.

Anne's experiences as a military wife taught her "how important it is for families to have both mom and dad around" (34). She also comes to believe that "soldiers and their families must be the people most devoted to peace since they feel the effects of war most directly" (34). One of these effects is made clear when one of their sons lies to his PE teacher about his father because he is "afraid he would cry in front of his friends if he told the truth, and to a fourteen-year-old boy that would have been horribly embarrassing" (39). Crying would also be a sign of disloyalty to his long-suffering father, and to the military's involvement in Vietnam.

This same son later applies to West Point, feeling that "by doing this he was honoring his father, perhaps helping him in some way" (128). One son threw himself into baseball while his father was interned. "When he played ball, he didn't have to think about his dad," Anne recounts. "His young mind was searching for something to replace his sadness" (131). Children of warriors suffer both when their fathers are absent—and when they return (if they *do* return). They can either wholeheartedly accept the military life for themselves, thereby never escaping the Fortress, or they can completely reject the warrior ethos of their household and the military community. Many Brats toggle between these two extremes: feeling proud and defensive of their fathers and feeling resentful and sometimes embarrassed about what they did for a living.

Moving away from the Vietnam experience, William Willis' 2013 *Base Jumping: The Vagabond Life of a Military Brat* tells of his life as the son of an Air Force father, who flew planes in World War II, worked in intelligence, and retired as a major. Although the tone of this memoir is often wryly humorous and sometimes positive about life as a Military Brat, it is also possible to detect the strains in this household. For example, when he tells his mother at age eight that he wants to be a jet pilot, "her face fell, and I knew I had struck a nerve.... She had tried her best to make me realize how tough that sort of life could be on a family: the constant moving and countless separations" (7–8). While his mother supports his father and the military mission, she dreads to think that her son might follow in his father's bootsteps.

Willis also describes an experience common to many Military Brats: the replication of the boot camp mentality at home, especially for the children of officers or senior enlisted. He says, "We were a squadron of two: Dad, the squad leader, and I, the lowly recruit. I sometimes felt like I was nothing more than Dad's obedient little soldier" (31). Willis does not blame his father, though: "He was a young father and junior officer who was so wrapped up in his own world that he thought what worked in the military should work in the family as well. How wrong he was!" (33).

Many military fathers, who often joined the service when they were still teenagers, incorrectly assume that the rigors of military training and discipline would be effective parenting strategies. Things were not always so regimented, though. Willis also enjoyed playing golf with his father, although no matter how much he relished his time with his father, he was "old enough to realize that, at any time, without warning, Uncle Sam could snatch him from me and make him disappear for months at a time on one of his secret spy missions" (109). This is the dilemma of the Brat: no matter how much one might enjoy these times, the specter of a mission always looms in the background.

In addition to the danger to the father from without, there is also danger *from* the father himself. When Willis and his teenage friend are caught in an off-limits enlisted soldiers' barracks, he worries about the effect on his father's career: "Base commanders didn't tolerate questionable behavior from their subordinates or their dependents. Neither did Dad—I got a pretty good whipping that night" (118). As this chapter has shown several times already, Military Brats not only have to worry about the personal consequences of their bad behavior; they must consider that their fathers' jobs might be on the line, which,

*One. "I rarely give up my vigilance"*

more often than not, ratchets up the punishment for what might seem to be minor offenses in the civilian world.

After his father retires and Willis becomes a teenager, he experiences feelings common to Brats when they leave the military life: "Gone were the days when I could move to a new town and fit in with ease and feel a sense of belonging.... I became a loner—an invisible entity who skirted the social scene like a ghost" (153). Consequently, at one point he tries to find the military housing where he had lived years before: "This place was the closest thing to roots I had ever had, and I needed that emotional connection like a drunk needing his next drink" (154). This is a common experience for the adult Brat, returning to a military base where he or she once lived to find "roots" or "emotional connection."

He also realizes how different he is from most of the people he encounters in adult life: "Kids who get to grow up in the same neighborhood will never understand the uncertainty and frustration of being uprooted every year—the sense of feeling that you don't quite fit in, always being targeted as the new kid on the block" (160). Feeling always like an outsider, always being the targeted "new kid on the block," was as painful for Willis as it has been for other Brats. Not surprisingly, Willis decides that he is not going to put his kids through that ordeal and pursues a career that will ensure that his children stay in the same neighborhood for their entire childhood.

These inherent conflicts in Brat life can be seen in two comments late in the autobiography. When Willis' father tells his son that his 22 years in the military "was one long party," his son thinks, "It wasn't a party for the Willis kids, and it definitely wasn't a party for Mom" (161). However, he follows this with that statement that he was "fortunate to be able to experience all the great amenities of base life that the government generously provided. I was also privileged to experience a variety of cultures and see parts of the world that most people only read about" (166). Once again, the Military Brat cannot admit, even to himself, that his experiences were consistently less than edifying.

This strange optimism in the face of prior experience can also be seen in Diane Ryan's 2015 *Child of the Blue: A Memoir of Growing Up Military*, in which she says "when the military called, our family answered. Once again, we said, 'Off we go'" (33). Willis and Ryan, along with many other Military Brats, seem to have a kind of negative capability about military life. They can clearly see the isolation, rigidity, violence, and secrecy that accompany life inside the Fortress, while at the same time they celebrate the excitement of a life that involves moving from place to place and the pride that comes with serving a higher purpose. Off we go, indeed, into a world in which we will never feel at home.

The most harrowing by far of these Brat autobiographies is Pat Conroy's 2014 *The Death of Santini*, in which he tells the "true" story of his father's life and death and the menacing presence he held in the household. It is a story, fictionalized in Conroy's 1978 *The Great Santini*, of verbal and physical child abuse, intimidation, chaos, and a deep and abiding sense of patriotism and sacrifice. (This novel will be discussed in a subsequent chapter.) However, trying to write such a book when the perpetrator of the violence is still alive can be deeply problematic. As Douglas says about narratives of trauma: "Autobiographies of childhood are necessarily relational; they become 'auto/biographies' conveying the life narratives of both the author and his or her parents" (131–32). According to Douglas, one cannot write just one's own story of trauma; one must have a victim and a perpetrator, and the perpetrator's story must be told as well. In this "auto/biography," Conroy tells both his story and the story of his father, and the son is, of course, the survivor, while his father is the perpetrator. The story he tells is one of both father and son, even though it is only told through the son's perspective.

In the prologue, Conroy jumps right in to tackle his father's anger, saying that its volatility and unpredictability was what made it dangerous. This anger is in large part due to his profession, Conroy wisely points out: "Because he was a fighter pilot of immense gifts, he was also born to kill" (5). This is the dangerous demand placed on military service men and women: they are asked to do their duty, which often means to kill for their country, and then, somehow, to come home and be loving and nurturing parents. Many are not able to make that shift, and the consequences for their children are enormous. As Conroy puts it, he wears his childhood "on my back like the carapace of a

## One. "I rarely give up my vigilance"

tortoise, except my shell burdens and does not protect. It weighs me down and fills me with dread" (11). Interestingly, the turtle metaphor is often used to console Brats who are required to move on a regular basis. Military children are told that they carry their homes on their backs to reconcile them to the frequent upheavals in their lives. However, as Conroy makes clear, this cozy carapace can also be a burden or prison. He extends these feelings to his brothers and sisters: "The Conroy children were all casualties of war, conscripts in a battle we didn't sign up for on the bloodied envelope of our birth certificates" (11). This is a truly horrifying image: the birth certificate is "bloodied" because the hands that legitimize the children have been steeped in the blood of enemies (and sometimes in the blood of their own children).

As critic Catherine Seltzer puts it in her book-length study of the author, Conroy's father "viewed his young family as he might a particularly disappointing series of recruits." Consequently, the Conroy siblings "were left with a paradoxical understanding of their father: on one hand, Don Conroy was a model of American masculinity, a true hero who served in three wars. On the other, he was a terrifying and abusive husband and father" (2). This comment neatly encapsulates the conflict of the Military Brat: one's father is a hero, without question, while at the same time he is a monster, a larger-than-life figure of fear and despair. And his children are perpetual "recruits" who fail, time and time again, to live up to the model their father sets for them, no matter how many times he tries to beat them into submission.

When writing his earlier novel, *The Great Santini*, Conroy says in this autobiography that he realizes that "there had been innumerable novels about soldiers and their wives and wartime, but I had never heard a word about the children. I was a proud member of an invisible tribe called 'military brats,' voiceless and unpraised as both children and adults" (62). *The Great Santini* and, later, *The Death of Santini*, were Conroy's ways of making that "invisible tribe" visible to the world—wounds and all. This "tribe" needed its stories told as well, even if not every Brat story is so violent and terrifying. The pride—and often the fear—go hand in hand in the Brat experience, as Conroy's stories show.

Without question, contradictions are part and parcel of Military

## Brat Life

Brat life. As Conroy says, "It had become clear that when Dad was gone, I was a happy young boy. When he was home, I became a melancholic, despairing one. Still, the return of the warrior was a rite of passage for every military brat on Earth" (63). Brats waiting for the military parent to return are filled with excitement—and with dread. The more relaxed regime that exists during the warrior's absence is brought to a screeching halt as the order-loving (and likely traumatized) soldier tries to assert his power over what he considers to be his now-unruly family. In addition, the family has no external stability with which to counter the often-violent reimposition of order when the father returns. As Seltzer puts it, "The enforced peripateticism of the Marine Corps ensured that the Conroy children never lived anywhere long enough to create a sense of stability to balance Don Conroy's volatility" (2). The Great Santini returns, and the family is powerless to stand up to the chaos swirling around him because they have no fixed place on which to stand.

In the book's epilogue, Conroy says, "The children of fighter pilots tell different stories than other kids do. None of our fathers can write a will or sell a life insurance policy or fill out a prescription or administer a flu shot or explain what a poet meant. We tell of our fathers who land on aircraft carriers at pitch-black night with the wind howling over the South China Sea" (330). These men are clearly heroes, but heroes do not always make the best family men. Seltzer says that Pat Conroy and his siblings "grew up in a house in which bravery and action were central tenets of an orthodox faith, yet Pat, along with his brothers and sisters, was forced into a position of passivity and silence throughout his childhood" (3). If one is living with a *bona fide* hero, one can only play the role of worshipper or slave.

Conroy says, "We were raised by the men who made the United States of America the safest country on earth in the bloodiest century in all recorded history" (331), and it is difficult to tarnish this image. Speaking to civilian children later in life, Conroy poignantly says, "Your fathers made communities like Beaufort [where *The Great Santini* is set and where Conroy eventually settled as an adult] decent and prosperous and functional; our fathers made the world safe for democracy" (331). Children can get their revenge, of a sort, on these

## One. "I rarely give up my vigilance"

larger-than-life men, though, by being an embarrassment to their father by wearing Birkenstocks, "flirting with vegetarianism" and voting for "candidates whom Dad would line up and shoot" (336). Thus, the only revenge a powerless child can have against his warrior father is to annoy and disappoint him—that is, unless one decides to go into the military and follow in his footsteps, which, in spite of his time at The Citadel, Pat Conroy was not about to do.

Conroy's story of his father's life has parallels with the trauma described by Jonathan Shay in his 1994 study of the psychological damage suffered by Vietnam Veterans, *Achilles in Vietnam.* A M.D. and Ph.D. staff psychologist in the Department of Veterans Affairs Outpatient Clinic in Boston, Shay sees men who are Vietnam veterans with severe PTSD. He argues that we should "learn how war damages the mind and spirit, and work to change those things in military institutions and cultures that needlessly create or worsen these injuries" (xxiii). Unhealed combat stress, he argues (and these autobiographies demonstrate), "costs, and costs, and costs" (195). It can, finally, "become a threat to democratic political institutions" (195), and it certainly is a threat to the family life and mental health of Military Brats.

What needs to be done, Shay says, is that our country must support returning soldiers on the home front *"regardless of ethical and political disagreements over the war itself"* (197, italics in the text). This support could include continuing unit cohesion after deployments to create a community after war time (198), Ultimately, "the official and folk culture of the American military must change so that grieving enjoys high status—is valued, not stigmatized" (198). These ideas, if implemented by the military, might have saved the Conroy children and countless other Brats from lives dominated by violent and depressed fathers.

Lt. Col. (ret.) Dave Grossman agrees. In his 1995 book, *On Killing: The Psychological Cost of Learning to Kill in War and Society* which was revised in 2009, Grossman, a retired Army Ranger, paratrooper, and psychology professor at West Point, says that "some psychiatric casualties have always been associated with war, but it was only in the twentieth century that our physical and logistical capability to sustain combat outstripped our psychological capacity to endure it" (45). The fathers that have been described in this chapter have all experienced 20th-century wars. In particular, Grossman says, "never in American history has the combination of psychological blows inflicted upon a group of returning warriors been so intense [as during the Vietnam War]" (282). He notes, as the Brat biographies from that period underscore, "Today we reap the legacy of those blows in a bitter harvest of PTSD in our Vietnam veterans" (282).

He notes, poignantly and angrily: "If society prepares a soldier to overcome his resistance to killing and places him in an environment in which he will kill, then society has an obligation to deal forthrightly, intelligently, and morally with the result and its repercussions upon the soldier and the society" (287). Society has a moral obligation, he is saying, to deal with the repercussions of training men to kill, and this also means dealing with the fallout in the families of these warriors. The cliché is that wounded people wound, and this is certainly true with the military: wounded soldiers (both physically and mentally) wound their spouses and children in ways that are just becoming clear to us today.

Finally, Grossman says that what Vietnam vets want and need is the "understanding that they did no more and no less than their nation and their society asked them to do; no more and no less than American veterans had honorably done for more than two centuries. And the simple affirmation that they are good human beings" (299). Veterans of all combat zones, but especially Vietnam, Afghanistan, and Iraq, need to be assured that they fought as honorably as soldiers of earlier wars, and that they are still "good human beings." Such attention to the common humanity of soldiers could go a long way toward healing the fractured lives of veterans and their children.

A good place to end this chapter is with Jennifer Sinor's incisive article "Inscribing Ordinary Trauma in the Diary of a Military Child." A Navy Brat, Sinor says that memoirs like the ones described in this chapter are "primarily an act of testimony, a public ritual of healing" (405). However, the question of who gets to tell such stories and what counts as war stories is contested. Military children's experiences are often not considered legitimate war stories: "For while they do not choose to serve, their lives, often from birth, are conscripted

## One. "I rarely give up my vigilance"

by the possibility and the paraphernalia of war.... In fact, to suggest that they have no war stories is to ignore one of the necessary costs of war" (407). As Brats and as children, these military offspring are "doubly disenfranchised" and often not seen as complicated characters in their own right (407–408). Brats are also seen by most people as recovering easily from the trauma of military life, as a result of their "remarkable flexibility and responsibility from an early age" (408).

Sinor stresses that "studying military children requires acknowledging their complicated positions and the cost for their service" (409). To understand the Military Brat, a good way to begin would be to look at the writing the children produced while still ensconced in the Fortress to learn about the "experiences of those conscripted by birth, rather than serving by choice, who do not fight in combat, but whose daily lives are nevertheless marked by war" (410). Sinor calls the experiences of Military Brats "ordinary trauma," by which she means "the extraordinary fact that one lives within a system dedicated to making war" (410). As with other trauma sufferers, little of this trauma is ever spoken, as it "must be actively and continually rendered ordinary, made perpetually invisible. Those who suffer from ordinary trauma do not and cannot name the extraordinariness of their situation because it is to them unexceptional" (410). Growing up on military bases surrounded by tanks, ships, planes, and/or submarines, not to mention weapons of all sorts, both at home and around the base, Military Brats learn to make the extraordinary into something ordinary, or, as Sinor says, "as common on military property as a fire hydrant or shrubbery" (411). They learn to see the extraordinary (including ordinary trauma) as ordinary.

The experience of Military Brats is different from that of their parents, Sinor says, "whose preservice memories can act as counter-narratives to military experience" (411). The ordinary but staggering effects of this constant preparation for war is the unacknowledged trauma of Brat life. Sinor puts this even more poetically: "Like its warships, the entire military community floats in a steady state of readiness" (417). Brats are also floating in this state of readiness—and fear.

Sinor says that she finds solace in conversations with other Brats, exchanges in which she is "struck by the familiarity of the experiences, which often appears at the level of language. For someone who had no home, these intersections become the closest thing I have to roots" (416). Giving herself "no justifiable room to be sad, scared, or lonely" (420), Sinor finds it "difficult to describe to anyone raised outside of the military the paradox of a military childhood" (422). Nevertheless, at the end of her book she vows to claim "ownership of the war story I tell here" (Sinor 422). This could be a call to testimony for other military children. Perhaps in the future they, too, can tell their stories.

While there are, according to Sinor, "some suggestions that the military is paying more attention to military dependents, and in particular to the health and wellbeing of military children"—including declaring 1984 "The Year of the Military Child," followed in 1986 by "The Year of the Military Family," and increasing services to military families (Note 7, 424)—there is still much work to be done, both inside and outside of the Fortress. Military families today struggle with the emotional burdens of frequent moves, isolation from extended families, and concerns for the dangers faced by the service member, and former Military Brats have difficulty making connections with those outside the military and finding a place to call home. Autobiographical narratives such as those by Conroy, Ryan, Steinman, Purcell, Gilberg, Hanna, and Arbuckle help Brats to feel less alone and more connected to their tough and resilient, repressed and hypervigilant, alienated and engaged tribe of warrior children.

# Two

# "Blanket of risk"
## Shorter Autobiographical Narratives

> "The good is that you always get to see new places, learn about foreign cultures ... and experience things which most people never have the opportunity in their lifetime. The bad is that you make friends fast ... and lose them even faster."
> —Marc Curtis, *Growing Up Military: Every Brat Has a Story* (NP)

Within the last few decades, several writers have collected shorter narratives of Brat life that explore a variety of perspectives about life inside the Fortress. These collections of comments by former Brats are, in general, more positive than the full-length autobiographies discussed in the previous chapter, but it is important to keep in mind they are subject to cutting and selection bias by the editors, which may contribute to their more positive tone. Deborah Harrison and Patrizia Albanese's 2016 *Growing Up in Armyville*, Marc Curtis' *Growing Up Military: Every Brat Has a Story* (2009), Deborah Ellis' 2008 *Off to War*, and Mary Truscott's *Brats* (1989) are examples of this relatively recent subgenre. While the individual comments are short, taken collectively, they may provide a more comprehensive (and perhaps more objective) picture of Brat life than either the fictional or book-length autobiographical works. On the other hand, they may also reflect the desires of the editors to present a certain upbeat view of Brat life.

In a slight departure from this book's focus on American military children, Harrison and Albanese's work is the result of a 2008 study of high-school-aged military children in a pseudonymous town in Canada whose parents were deployed to Afghanistan. Drawing on recent studies of a variety of Canadian families, Harrison and Albanese determined that while almost every Canadian family experiences some sort of stress, "military families experience more stressors than their share." These conflicts, they say, could be from economic hardship, familial disruptions, and interpersonal conflict (25). According to a recent Canadian military ombudsman's report, the authors say, "three key stressors shape the lives of military members and their families: geographic relocations, frequent separations due to training and deployments, and living under a blanket of risk" as a result of the military parent's career (29). This coincides with the data included in the Introduction and the individual autobiographical narratives in Chapter One, which show that the children of military members are under stress from various elements intrinsic to Brat life.

Perhaps most significant for Military Brats, people serving in the military and their dependents in Canada and the United States are often separated from extended family, which increases their isolation and leads them to rely on other military families for support (31). Despite support from their fellow Brats and their military community, however, "adolescents who have experienced a large number of family deployments over the past 10 years and have moved frequently," Harrison and Albanese say, "have been found to be more likely to have been victimized by their peers and/or to have carried weapons [as well as used substances like alcohol, tobacco and marijuana and had] more depressive symptoms, lower academic performance, and lower persistence" (34). This suggests, at the very least, that military support systems for Brats are not as effective as they might be, especially for Brats for whom a parent is deployed frequently and whose family moves often.

Other stressors on Brats included *"parental emotional unavailability"* (35, emphasis in the original) on the part of the parent left at home during deployment. This emotional detachment often results in the *"parentification* of older children and adolescents" (35, emphasis in the original), as those children assume caretaking and emotional support duties for their younger siblings and, sometimes, their remaining parent. These stressors, which often result in turning children into caretakers and surrogate parents, have been noted throughout the works examined in this book.

After deployment ends, family reunions can be equally difficult, as military members of the family, Harrison and Albanese say, "must reintegrate into homes whose internal rhythms have changed, and where both children and spouses have taken on new roles" (36). Families have been changed by deployment, and they remain so when the service member returns and things get back to "normal." In addition, "members returning from overseas experience complicated emotions related to what they may have witnessed, especially if they were injured or were present at the injuries or deaths of comrades or civilians. They return to what they often perceive to be mundane matters, and they may be anxious about their ability to carry out their parenting and household roles in the ways they did before" (135). A military parent returning from war finds it almost impossible to attend to mundane household tasks and may suffer from anxiety and outbursts related to PTSD. In addition, family or intimate-partner violence is both "unresearched and underreported" in military families, suggesting that much of what happens behind the closed doors of the family is unavailable to researchers (38). Thus, the stresses of absence are often matched by the stresses of reunion, despite all the sentimental pictures of families joyfully reuniting with their deployed parents and the paeons to the resilience of Military Brats.

Despite these tensions, the researchers found that "the mental well-being of CAF [Canadian Armed Forces] adolescents attending AHS [the pseudonymous 'Armyville High School'] was no worse than that of their civilian school peers" (47). However, that conclusion seems undercut, especially for female Brats, by the researchers' other finding that "the lion's share of the extra emotional work [comforting and caretaking the younger children and undeployed parent] carried out was done by the girls" (107). In addition, girls "carried out the emotional work of censoring the information they conveyed to the parent who was deployed, to prevent him/her from worrying about what was happening at home and to keep him/her able to focus on the dangerous work s/he was doing" (108). Unsurprisingly, it falls to the girls in the family to do the emotional (and often physical) work needed to keep the family sane and whole. These are the same girls whose contributions are often devalued in a male-oriented military family. Female Brats seem to get all of the work and none of the glory.

Much of what Harris and Albanese noted in their study is corroborated in Marc Curtis' *Growing Up Military: Every Brat Has a Story*. This self-published work is connected to the Military Brats Registry (militarybrat.com), which was begun by Curtis in 1997 after he read Mary Wertsch's book. Curtis wanted to create a clearinghouse for Brats and a way for them to find old friends and discover a stronger sense of community, and the book is a compilation of responses by Brats on the website. Curtis speaks for many Brats when he talks about the frequent moving, which he says was good and bad: "The good is that you always get to see new places, learn about foreign cultures (Texas is quite foreign), and experience things which most people never have the opportunity in their lifetime. The bad is that you make friends fast … and lose them even faster" (NP). Brats learn to make friends quickly, and they value their varied life experiences, but they also learn that nothing is permanent and that they do not really belong anywhere. This good/bad dynamic corroborates what many Brats report in both their autobiographical and fictional accounts of life inside the Fortress.

One of the contributors to Curtis' book is Sandy Maghan, who concurs with the positive aspects: Military Brat life, she says, "opened up so much for my brothers and me. We saw things that most other children our age had not even read about" (NP). This is a common feeling for Brats: their frequent travel leads them to believe that they are unique in their broader perspectives on the world and superior to civilian children who remain in the same home/location for their entire childhoods. Jan Wertz agrees, saying that being an Air Force Brat "means I can make myself at home anywhere yet have no one place to call home. No friends, or family except for my parents, who I have known all my life. I have a larger frame of reference—and enjoy it. I can't say it is entirely an unmixed blessing, but I wouldn't trade being a Military Brat for growing up a rooted-in-one-place person" (NP). While she admits, diplomatically, that being a Brat is not "entirely an unmixed blessing," Wertz insists that she "wouldn't trade" it for a life

## Two. "Blanket of risk"

being "rooted-in-one-place." Civilians, and their children, are mired in one place, she implies; Brats have broader frames of reference and by implication have better judgment about the world. Also on the positive side, military children in Curtis' book reported a sense of pride in their fathers: "I knew my Dad was more than just a Dad. He was an American Soldier and so proud of it," said Cindi Van Liew (NP). This echoes what Pat Conroy has said about his father and what other Brats report feeling: their fathers may be strict, absent, volatile, and sometimes violent, but they are "more than just a Dad." Heroes, after all, are forgiven their clay feet and their sometimes-violent outbursts.

Other Brats in Curtis' book were less positive. Marina Hardy said that she learned "how to assume the local protective coloring as quickly as possible. It was a matter of survival, so I learned to talk like the locals, dress like the locals, and act like the locals—at least enough not to be singled out" (NP). This code-switching is a necessary skill for children who find themselves in new environments (and sometimes in new countries) every few years. The downside to this was that Hardy says she "always felt different and set apart on the inside even if I could pass for a local on the outside. I had no true sense of place or of belonging." Brats try to fit in, as a matter of survival, but in doing so they hide their authentic selves from friends, loved ones, and even their families.

Larry Jones explores another unintended consequence of inhabiting the Fortress: that his family and the others around him "lived in tiny, cookie-cutter Capehart housing in housing areas on a base surrounded by fences and barbed wire and guarded by young boys in uniforms with real M-16s. We also had a flight line covered with B-52's, each armed with nuclear weapons that could destroy the world. None of this seemed extraordinary or even odd" (NP). As Wertsch and others have noted, living surrounded by the implements of war becomes ordinary, although it is more like what Jennifer Sinor calls an "ordinary trauma." That is, while the implements of war all around them often go unnoticed, they provide subconscious reminders of the precariousness of their existence. Boys guarding nuclear weapons with guns, war planes adjacent to neighborhoods, and tanks rolling down streets are all common sights on military bases, where Brats and their families live, attend church, go to movies, swim, and shop for groceries. They know that their mission is violent, and yet they come to accept the threat and try to continue on with their ordinary, traumatic lives.

Mostly poignantly, Brats worry about being invisible, both to their civilian peers and to the world of the military. Linda Griffin says that she hopes that recent dependents' "contributions are recognized; ours were not" (NP). Brats, while they seem to be more often recognized (at least on billboards on military bases), often feel as if no one appreciates—or even notices—the very real sacrifices they were forced to make. Rarely, if ever, is a Brat thanked for his or her 18-year service to the country. As has been noted earlier, female Brats are even less likely to have their contributions acknowledged, even if they bear a heavier responsibility of caretaking. It is hoped that one effect of this book is that the contributions Brats make to the military will be recognized, and that Griffin and other Brats will finally be thanked for their service.

Deborah Ellis' 2008 *Off to War: Voices of Soldiers' Children* captures some of the tensions and contradictions explored in Curtis' book and Harrison and Albanese's study. It begins with an epigraph from the *Parent Guidebook, US Army Secondary Education Transition Study,* which notes that while the common understanding of military children is that they are resilient kids who have unique and rewarding experiences, "they are children first and connected to the military second." This is, of course, the ideal. However, Ellis reminds readers that part of the cost of war "is being paid by the military families who are left behind, especially the children" (10). Yes, military children become resilient because they must be, and they do have "unique and rewarding experiences," but it is not often that Brats are treated as children first and dependents second. As Ellis reminds us, children pay a price for living inside the Fortress, and in any war, "it is always children who are the biggest losers—children whose voices are rarely heard" (11). In this book, Ellis interviews children aged seven to 17 whose parents are currently service men and women in the United States and Canada, with the aim of having their voices finally heard.

Matt, 16, says that he has "gotten used to the transition of [his father] leaving. Now I hardly even think about it. There's more responsibility put on me. I have to assume, to some degree, the role of the

## Two. "Blanket of risk"

father figure" (14). Matt is experiencing the "parentification" reported by Harrison and Albanese, which includes having to take on the role of "father figure" and do many of the household chores his father would have done. He also experiences the self-denial: "I have to think of the family as a whole to make it all work," he says. "If I only thought of myself, then the whole family would be miserable, which would make me miserable, so I wouldn't be happy anyway" (15). Even though he is only 16, Matt, like other Brats, feels as if it is his strength of will and sacrifice that holds the family together. If his family is not happy, he cannot be happy.

Kaylee, 13, talks about her mom's frenzied cleaning sprees after her father leaves (84), and Matthew, 11, says that it is hard to talk about the time when his father was deployed and his mother was "mostly really angry or really sad. I tried to keep myself away from conflict and bad emotions, but I wasn't always successful" (101). Military children like Kaylee and Matthew frequently witness the troubling responses that the at-home parent experiences, and they often feel that they must make things right and/or prevent conflict. They also must cope with their own emotions. Nine-year-old Ashley says that she has learned to calm herself down: "When I get worried, I take a lot of deep breaths and say, 'He's going to be okay. Everything's going to be okay.' Most of the time I can make myself believe it" (137).

The only other children than Brats who worry on a regular basis that their parents will "be okay" are those who live with adults who suffer from physical or mental illness or substance use disorder. Clearly, military children experience many of the Adverse Childhood Experiences (ACEs) that psychologists are using to determine whether an adult will suffer from various psychological, social, and physical ailments. The difference is that they are told by their parents and by the military that these stressors are necessary for the protection of the nation (and even the world).

These feelings of fear, sadness, and grown-up responsibility are exacerbated by the isolation of military families from extended family networks that Harrison and Albanese have observed in their study: "The army moves people around the world," Matt says. "Our nearest relative is thirteen hours away. You have to rely on your military family" (18). Relying on the military "family" is certainly better than nothing, but while they might understand the peculiar stresses that Brats experience, families of service members are experiencing similar struggles and may not have the emotional bandwidth to help others outside their own families. Dylan, 11, says that his family was sad when his father, whom he describes as "one of the good ones," who does not "drink or yell or hit a lot," was deployed. "Mom was always up in her room the first time [his father was deployed], with the baby, and she was sad, so I had to do lots of extra things for my brother and sister so they wouldn't bother her and would let her rest. A lot of the time my brother and sister were even too sad to play. The whole house was sad for a long time" (111). This is heartbreaking: a household in which the children were "too sad to play," and where an 11-year-old is charged with keeping his siblings quiet and ensuring his mother's peace of mind. Patrick, 14, says that having his father gone is a "big loss for our family because he's a really big factor in keeping our family going" (128). A military father is a powerful figure, one who creates the structures and the rules that govern his family. When he is gone, the routines are disrupted; families often wonder what to do with themselves. As has been mentioned earlier, though, reuniting can be equally difficult, as the service member resents his diminished place in the household and the mundanity of ordinary life.

Despite all these stressors, military children often learn to underplay their anxiety and depression. Allison, 11, advises Military Brats not to "overdramatize when your parents are going overseas. If you do, you'll just make it harder for yourself because you'll be so worried you could actually make yourself sick. Find someone you can trust if you need to talk to someone, like your mom, or your pastor, or a friend, or a school guidance counselor. Find some way to relieve your stress. You have your own life to live" (21). It is difficult to imagine an 11-year-old with such preternatural self-restraint, but it is a common mindset of Military Brats, regardless of their age, that one must always have a stiff upper lip and pretend that nothing out of the ordinary is happening when one's parent is sent to a war zone for months at a time. Counselors or pastors may be available, but military children are often cautioned not to air the family's dirty laundry to outsiders. Nine-year-old

## Two. "Blanket of risk"

Lewis's comment is even more heartbreaking. He says his family has gotten *used* to his father's absences: "He misses most holidays. He misses everyone's birthday, even his own" (20). Family celebrations become reminders of the missing parent, and to avoid the pain, children learn to get used to the father or mother being gone.

Even when the military parent is home, he often is not emotionally present. Mikayla, 12, says that before her father left for overseas "he was funny, and he would play around with us a lot. He'd joke around or play cards with us, and do all these things with us. He doesn't play with us anymore now, not really. He spends most of his time on the computer, looking up photographs. Or watches TV" (51). As the returning service member struggles to understand what he has experienced in a war zone, he often withdraws from family life, preferring to spend time with the computer or the television. That funny, playful father has become distant and distracted. Sometimes the reality of Brat life is even harsher. A 17-year-old responding anonymously says, "Dad moved from just yelling and screaming to being physically abusive again, hitting me, shoving me down the hallway, blocking me and bullying me. He threatened to flush my pets down the toilet" (150). A traumatized parent can—and often does—inflict trauma on his or her children, and this intergenerational trauma can be seen clearly in the longer fictional and nonfictional narratives of Brat life discussed in this book. Pat Conroy, and his fictional alter ego, had many such violent encounters with "The Great Santini."

In addition to the violence and emotional distance of the military parent, Brats experience stress from the civilian community. Kaela, 13, comments on the isolation from peers that many Military Brats feel: "Civilian kids don't understand anything," she says. When she stayed out of school because she was sad about her father's absence, the kids teased her. She also reports feeling sick and "worried and nervous" when her father is gone and that she could not concentrate on schoolwork even when she was able to go (44). As fewer and fewer military children attend schools on base (as most of these DOD schools have closed), there is often no one in the civilian school—student or teacher—who can understand what these children are experiencing. Erika, 17, says that she would not talk to her friends, even if they were

## Brat Life

Brats, "because I wouldn't want to cry in front of them" (62). To cry is to admit weakness, which would give rise to fear, and, perhaps, could be seen as a kind of disloyalty to the country that has sent the military member to war.

Along this line, Tori, 11, finds it "strange" to be with nonmilitary kids "because they can live their lives without a clue about what's going on in the world. Some of them barely know who the president is, let alone that there's a war going on. So there is me, with my father far away and maybe getting shot at or dying for his country, and there's these regular kids who don't have a clue." Military Brats often feel that they have a better understanding of world events than their civilian peers, in large part because the lives of their loved ones depend upon those events. Civilian children do not need to be attuned to the latest goings on in the Middle East, for example. However, Tori adds that it is "good to have non-military friends, though. It helps me feel normal. If all you had were army kids for friends, you could never forget about the world, and sometimes it's good to forget for a little while" (122). Socializing with nonmilitary friends can be therapeutic, since one does not have to talk about the fear and loss on the margins—and sometimes front and center—of Brat life, but, again, this means hiding what may feel like the truest part of oneself from one's friends.

In general, Brats' takeaway from their time as military children is the high cost associated with being a military child, and many of them choose to avoid enlisting in the services themselves out of concern for the trauma it might inflict on their future children. Santana, 12, says there are several reasons that she would not want to join the military: "My mom works with military families and she sees what happens to them—things like divorce, and people coming back from the war injured, or not coming back at all. I do not want to be a part of that" (29). What Santana seems to be saying is that she does not want to pass the trauma of a military childhood on to future generations. Ashley, nine, says she "can't think about anything that's good about being in a military family. I know I won't join the army. Why would I want to do something that would take me away from my family?" (133). Ashley asks a poignant question: Why would anyone want to do that to their kids? This, of course, implies that it should not have

## Two. "Blanket of risk"

been done to her. Even more tragically than Ashley, Patrick, 12, whose father was killed in Iraq, says that his advice for other military kids is "I don't have any. I'm not a military kid anymore" (165). This is one of the harshest realities of military life: if the service member is killed, the children must leave the only life that they have ever known. They cannot stay on base, and they are often forced to return to extended family from whom they have become estranged over the years of moving from duty station to duty station. His only identity—that of Military Brat—has been precipitously taken from him.

To a lesser degree, this banishment happens eventually to all Military Brats, although if they are "lucky," it will not happen until they are 18 and are no longer considered dependents. Mary R. Truscott, who wrote *Brats: Children of the American Military Speak Out*, talks about this aspect of Brat life from within a family that produced both the World War II General Lucian Truscott,, Jr., and the novelist Lucian Truscott IV: "I left home and left the military behind. I have only infrequently discussed the details of my background with anyone other than my immediate family. Even when I've met other military brats, once we establish the commonality of our backgrounds, we rarely discuss our experiences: we just assume that they were similar" (2). As Truscott says, when military children reach 18, they are no longer able to access the installations where they grew up, and they inevitably lose contact with the other Brats, who have scattered to the four winds. She accurately points out that a military career "defines and shapes the lives of families to an extent that is rarely matched in nonmilitary occupations.... Military life includes frequent moves, and the ensuing isolation from relatives and friends, a father's long- or short-term absences from home, and risks that are an inescapable part of military duty during war or peacetime" (3). The bottom line is that former Brats have no one with whom they can—or are willing to—share their particularly traumatic experiences.

This is in part because of what many Brats in this study have noted, that military families, as Truscott puts it, "keep closed ranks; they mind their own business. I believe that the tendency to close ranks is particularly common in military families: life on a post is often compared to life in a goldfish bowl. Any hint of family problems, even in casual conversation, could have an impact on a family's reputation, and ultimately, on a father's career" (4). Again, Brats live on that stage that Wertsch describes, one that has life-or-death consequences, and, as a result, it would be dangerous to share too many of their experiences with outsiders. The "goldfish bowl" is another way of describing the sense that Brats have that while they are protected from the outside world, they are also on display 24/7. To continue the metaphor, they also find that they cannot breathe in the air of civilian life, even when they find themselves thrust into it at 18.

Truscott also notes that when moving from military installation to military installation, her family "had no home to return to, and no idea of what our home would be like. We saw enormous stretches of the United States from the backseat of the car, free and unfettered" (26). This could sound positive: the family on the open road, taking in the vastness of the country, headed to a new adventure. However, this ignores the essential unreality of military life. The houses that they lived in were merely "stage sets, scenic backdrops" (27), with nothing feeling permanent or dependable. This supports Mary Wertsch's observations about the essential theatricality of military life: one is always on stage, always on the move, and never attached to any one place or any particular group of people (except for one's immediate family). "The sets changed frequently," Truscott says, "but our props, carefully packed and unpacked, never varied" (27).

These vignettes of Brat life corroborate what the longer autobiographies have asserted: Brats are often isolated, overly parentified, and frequently frightened, both of what might happen if a parent never returns—and what is likely to happen when he does. Brats experience the world in ways that civilian children might not; they learn to be resilient and to ignore the preparations for war going on all around them, but they do so at the cost of connections to their extended families, a sense of place, long-term friendships, and even the basic security of knowing their parents will be present and emotionally available for them. The fictional narratives discussed in subsequent chapters will expand on these issues in sometimes entertaining and frequently disturbing ways, but there is power and connection in hearing one's stories being told.

## Three

# "Our fathers are military officers first, and fathers second"
### *Young Adult Novels of Brat Life*

> We became quiet as bivalves at his approach and our lives were desperate and sad. But when the United States needed a fighter pilot, we did our best to provide one. Our contribution to the country was small, but so were we most of the time, and we gave all that we could.
> —Pat Conroy, "Introduction" to *Military Brats*, xvii

Novels intended for adults and first-person, nonfiction narratives about Brat Life—like Pat Conroy's novel *The Great Santini* and biography of his Marine pilot father *The Death of Santini*—offer reflections on the pleasures, traumas, and inconveniences of life as military children; young adult novels, written from the perspective of adolescents, provide unique insights for their young readers. Written from 2000 to 2017, the works discussed below imagine an audience of Military Brats who might see their own experiences reflected in the stories, but they also reach out to the wider civilian community and provide glimpses into the often-hidden world inside the Fortress.

The novels discussed in this chapter, Daphne Benedis-Grab's *Army Brats* (2017), Ashlee Cowles' *Beneath Wandering Stars* (2016), Vicki Bohe-Thackwell's *Too Skinny to Float* (2000), Frances O'Roark Dowell's *Shooting the Moon* (2010), Roseanne Parry's *Heart of a*

## Brat Life

*Shepherd* (2009), Sara Lewis Holmes' *Operation YES* (2009), and Michael Joseph Lyon's *Brat and the Kids of Warriors* (2017), treat the experiences of Military Brats lightheartedly (and somewhat unrealistically), dramatically, movingly, satirically, and, finally, critically. Most are written by people who have had direct experience with life in the military, and they effectively capture the complexities, contradictions, worries, and joys of such a life. They feature both male and female protagonists, who are aged from 10 to 17, and while some of the minor characters are African American or Asian, for the most part these are the experiences of white children, who are primarily the offspring of white officers or senior enlisted. They are moving and funny, poignant and patriotic, scary and sardonic. Throughout them all runs a common love of country and dedication to (at least on the surface) being the best Brats possible.

These novels approach children's and young adults' experiences during the 1950s and 1960s occupation of Germany, the Vietnam War era in the 1970s, and the wars in Afghanistan and Iraq in the 1990s and 2000s. Their protagonists also run the gamut from gung-ho children, who become skeptical and rebellious adolescents, to grieving survivors, and to boys and girls finding adventure on the relatively safe confines of military bases at home and abroad. In all the novels, common themes are present: the foundational secrecy of Brat life, the necessity to represent the nation positively, the strict (but often ignored) division of children by the ranks of their fathers or mothers, the frequent disruptions of homes and friendships, the ever-present fear of loss, the violence and dysfunction of many military families, the familiarity and comfort of the rituals, and, perhaps most importantly to many of the characters (and perhaps authors), the overarching sense of purpose of military life.

They differ from the adult novels and memoirs, however, because they often provide a sense of hope, or at least open-endedness, in their conclusions. They fit into a common model for YA fiction that tends to take into consideration the age and experiences of its readers. Beyond that, though, it is sometimes difficult to define just what makes these works adolescent fiction, other than the ways in which they are marketed on book covers and in bookstores. Scholar of adolescent

## Three. "Military officers first, and fathers second"

literature Mike Cadden says that both children's and young adult novels are "fuzzy sets, culturally and structurally protean like the novel" (303), but he adds that their "indeterminacy" allows them to "stay relevant and alive in culture" (303). Perhaps simply their varying perspectives on child and young adulthood and optimistic endings are what mark them as adolescent fiction.

Certainly, novels like these, which look at the Brat experience through both comic and tragic modes, are both "relevant and alive," regardless of their often more hopeful (and sometimes idealistic) conclusions. As Cadden says, YA novels are usually "about change and growth" (310), with the goals being "the triumph of the unified self able to grow, the integration of a self partly determined by society, or the discovery of a self (self-consciousness) that is almost purely socially determined" (310). The common thread, it seems, is some sort of growth and development of the self, as well as the positionality of the self in society. Indeed, Cadden says, a tension exists in these novels "between the desire to create a romantic figure in search of self and of depicting society as the inscriber of the adolescent self" (310). In other words, this development can be framed or even harmed by the larger society in which the protagonists live. With YA novels about military children, this tension is especially pronounced, as the adolescent protagonists struggle between their personal desires and the needs (or, rather, the requirements) of military life.

This conflict can be managed skillfully or formulaically, according to Cadden. Novels that exhibit what Cadden, borrowing from Ursula K. Le Guin, calls "fake realism" often invoke "scripted and formulaic transformations. They give the reader what she wants, as romance does, but without earning it through building superior characters, in whatever way, who succeed believably" (311). While this sort of false verisimilitude might appeal to parents who want to reinforce the virtues of self-sacrifice demanded by life in the military, it inevitably "entices young readers to wallow in unrealistic expectations about their lives as well as others" (311). Several of the novels discussed below exhibit, at least in part, some of these qualities of "fake realism." While it is, of course, difficult to ascribe motives to writers (not that this has not been done since time immemorial by literary critics), it may be possible to say that YA fiction about Military Brats that results in the main character coming to accept all aspects of life inside the Fortress is both unrealistic and damaging to its readers. The underlying message is that children who push back against the frequent moves, the absent parents, the sense of impending threat that surrounds them, and the overall silence in the face of their concerns are somehow flawed and need to reconcile themselves to the inevitable, which is constructed as putting the mission ahead of the individual.

Roberta Trites is also concerned about the conformist message of YA fiction, although she would not confine it to poorly crafted adolescent novels. As she puts it, unlike in children's literature, "growth in adolescent literature is inevitably depicted as a function of what the adolescent has learned about how society curtails the individual's power" (473). Thus, the development in YA novels moves toward integrating and subsuming the adolescent into the society in which he or she lives. While I question whether this is the case with all YA fiction, it does seem that this is the function of many adolescent novels directed toward Brat readers. Trites says that YA fiction shows its readers that adolescents "must learn to negotiate the many institutions that shape them ... to balance their power with their parents' power and with the power of authority figures in general ... [and] learn what portion of power they wield because of and despite such biological imperatives as sex and death" (473). Negotiating the various kinds of adult power becomes the adolescent's primary task. For the Military Brat, this is an especially difficult challenge, as the "power of authority figures" is the power of the State, embodied in the uniformed presence of a parent.

Gail Murray agrees, arguing that literature for children "is a conservative medium. Clergy, teachers, parents, and writers have all used it to shape morals, control information, model proper behavior, delineate gender roles, and reinforce class, race, and ethnic separation. Historically, children's fiction has not encouraged creativity, exploration of behaviors, or self-expression" (xvi). This is a perfect definition of the function of the Military Industrial Complex on the children and young adults that grow up under its wing (or in its shadow). Self-expression is not a character trait prized by the military—not in its service men and

### Three. "Military officers first, and fathers second"

women, nor in the spouse whose job it is to support the service member, nor in the children, whose duty it is to be obedient, not to bring shame on the service member, and to accept the frequent dislocations of military life with grace and good humor.

According to Eric Tribunella, loss, and its accompanying trauma, are frequently used in children's fiction "as a way of provoking or ensuring the development of children." This pattern of putting children or young adults in peril, he says, "suggests that children's literature, and indeed American culture, relies on the contrived traumatization of children—both protagonists and readers—as a way of representing and promoting the process of becoming a mature adult." He continues: "It is as if loss generates the escape velocity of youth. It is the fuel used to achieve the speed necessary for escaping the gravitational force of childhood" (xi). Trauma, transformation, escape: this is the pattern for the main characters in children's and young adult literature.

For young adult fiction in particular, Tribunella says, "the depiction and inducement of traumatic loss and knowledge are hallmarks" (53). In the lives of Military Brats, trauma is an everyday fact of life: parents, under the stresses of deployment and/or injury, can become abusive; children can lose caregivers temporarily and sometimes permanently; and none of this trauma can be shared, even within the family. Any sign of weakness or discontent is seen as damaging to the overall mission of protecting the nation. As a recent study of the psychological lives of military children reports: "Children in military families can experience elevated rates of trauma and mental health difficulties.... Studies involving military children show that repeated or lengthy deployments may result in attachment disturbances" (Hathaway et al. 55). Clearly, traumatic experiences are part and parcel of Brat life. However, applying Tribunella's model to YA fiction about Military Brats is challenging, since the trauma is rarely specifically focused or time delimited. Brats live the potential for loss and violence daily; there is no chance to absorb the experience and be transformed by it in positive ways.

However, young adult fiction that honestly explores this "ordinary trauma," as Sinor terms it, can provide a validation of the feelings of its readers and a sense of not being alone in what feels like an intensely personal drama. As Kay Vandergrift says, "Engagement with story is life-affirming; it puts us in touch with the world, with one another, and with our essential selves. Story also empowers readers to create wholeness, to make meanings that unify our own fragmented experiences and ideas with those expressed in story" ("Introduction" ix). To engage with the stories of other Brats can allow military children—both past and present—to "create wholeness" and to find a context into which they can place their experiences. Simply knowing that one is not alone can be beneficial.

In sum, books that young people read matter. As Carol Collins says, books read by young adults "have power. Their power rests in their ability to sway and to change the reader in so many ways, not the least of these is morally. These books can create a moral sense in the young by demonstrating what is morally right and what is morally wrong. They can raise and resolve ethical issues. The reader may not agree with each resolution, but is certainly forced to think about issues he or she may never have thought about before" (181). The hope is that these books, often written by and frequently directed to Military Brats, can encourage their readers both to come to terms with and to raise questions about their lives in the Fortress.

Daphne Benedis-Grab's *Army Brats* (2017) is designed for younger readers and has an essentially comic plot, but it does touch on many of the realities of Brat life. It also adds the more atypical element of the service person being the mother, not the father. In this novel, the Bailey family, including 12-year-old Tom, 10-year-old Charlotte, six-year-old Rosie, and Cupcake the dog, have moved onto an Army post for the first time. Their mother is a psychologist who is in military intelligence, and who has returned recently from a deployment overseas. This makes this novel relatively unusual, given that the service member is the mother, not the father; the father takes care of the children when Mom is away.

The novel has a *Scooby Doo* plot about a mysterious stranger, an abandoned building, and a clandestine military working dogs' reentry program, which is all resolved happily at the end. According to the acknowledgments, the author has cousins who grew up on Army

## Three. "Military officers first, and fathers second"

bases and consulted friends "for fine-tuning the army-related lingo and facts." Unfortunately, her "fine-tuning" does not reflect many of the realities of Brat life and even creates some highly improbable scenarios. More importantly, it suggests that most of Brat life consists of adventures and minor forms of disobedience that result in few—if any—negative consequences. Consequently, it may be the most lighthearted, and most unrealistic, of the novels discussed in this chapter.

Still, it does touch on some of the uncomfortable facts of Brat life, in particular the frequent moves and the experience, repeated multiple times, of entering a new school. From Charlotte's point of view, "No matter how often it happened, it was hard to leave friends and the familiar behind for a new, uncertain future. The one thing that made the moves easier, of course, was her siblings. They might fight sometimes, but walking into school on the first day was always a million times easier with Tom by her side" (3–4). The importance of siblings in the life of a Brat cannot be overstated: when one is leaving friends behind every few years and has little contact with extended family, siblings become the only reliable anchor.

These personal struggles are juxtaposed with the "familiar swell of pride that always blossomed inside" when Charlotte hears her mother talking about work: "Lots of moms had cool jobs, but their mom was a major in the US Army, protecting their country, and it didn't get any cooler than that" (9). Of course, part of Mom's "cool job" is using her skills to extract information from prisoners of war and anticipating the behaviors of foreign combatants, but this is never explored in the novel. Consistently, the author juxtaposes something problematic about life as a Brat with a patriotic or comic moment.

Another aspect of Brat life discussed in this ambiguous way in the novel is living on the post (or base, as it is referred to by the Navy and Air Force). While the kids are told they will have more freedom of movement on post, military installations are the ultimate gated community, guarded not just by unarmed security guards or key-carded gates but by armed Military Police checking IDs at the only available entrances, which are also barricaded and responsive in real time to threats at home and abroad. As the family approaches the post's gates, their mother speaks to the kids in "the voice that reminded them that she was an officer in the United States Army," telling them, "'On post we follow the rules, always and no matter what. You guys are going to have a lot more independence living at Fort Patrick, but you need to use that freedom wisely'" (11). Freedom always comes at a cost, as the children of the military know all too well. As Mary Truscott, the daughter of a World War II Army general whose work was featured in the previous chapter, puts it, "Uncle Sam was merely another distant relative, an invisible man who dominated every aspect of our lives" (11). This "invisible man" surveils and reports to superiors about every movement and action of the people within his borders.

This external surveillance and control are quickly internalized, and, as they approach the gates, Tom feels that "he *was* a member of an army family and wanted to look like it" (12). What might be greeted by incredulity or mockery by civilian children becomes part of the identity and psychology of Brats. Driving into what Tom calls "a modern-day fortress" (12), Tom notices, "As would be expected on an army post, each yard had neatly trimmed grass and carefully tended flower beds without a single weed in sight" (15). Nothing is wrong, per se, with "neatly trimmed grass and carefully tended flower beds," but this indicates that the level of control on military bases extends even to lawn care. Another harsh reality of Brat life is the anxiety associated with parental deployment, or as Charlotte puts it, "barely seeing Mom and worrying every night about whether she would come home at all" (37). In addition, there is the ongoing fear that if you misbehave, especially on a military base, "they call your army parent's commanding officer" (43). Fear—of the loss of a parent to deployment or death, of shaming one's parents and thereby somehow damaging the military mission, of not being a good enough representative of the United States—dominates Brat life.

In addition to fear, the theatrical side of military life on base that Wertsch describes is also present in this novel. The "Retreat" ceremony at 5:00 p.m. every day when the flag is lowered gives Charlotte "shivers." Her mother says "that even after all her years of 'Retreat' in the evening, 'Reveille' in the morning, and 'Taps' late at night, she still got chills every time she stopped and took a few minutes to honor

*Three. "Military officers first, and fathers second"*

the flag" (87). These musical punctuations of daily life on a military base remind residents of their mission from the moment they wake up until the moment they fall asleep; they are the overture and the finale to life inside the Fortress. In addition, Rose is reminded while at the post movie theater that "before they start previews, everyone stands up for 'The Star-Spangled Banner,' like at a ball game" (184). Even if one is riding one's bike after school or going to a Saturday matinee, one is never allowed to forget that one's first duty is to one's country. The pleasures of childhood are imbued with a heavy—but not always unpleasant—sense of responsibility.

Despite having spent their previous lives outside of this theatrical world of the military base, the children quickly and seamlessly adapt to life on post until they notice a strange man whose "steps [were] haphazard and unmilitary-like, his shoulders stooped" (176). In response to this stoop-shouldered, clearly unmilitary intruder, "Charlotte stood tall, in proper army style, straightened her umbrella, and strode toward him" (177). Imitating the posture of a soldier, Charlotte attempts to intimidate the stranger into behaving properly—or into leaving. By this point in the novel, Charlotte has completely absorbed the protocols of post life, and she fears any adult whose role is not clearly defined by his clothing and posture. This mysterious and "haphazard" stranger turns out to be involved with the dog-training operation, however, which the children "uncover" at the end of the novel.

While the plot is fanciful, Brat life, and the emotions associated with it, are true to life. However, one incident in the novel seems particularly unrealistic (and is perhaps the best evidence that Benedis-Grab did not spend much time on a military installation) is when Rosie shouts "IED" [shorthand for Improvised Explosive Device] in the PX [Post Exchange, the military equivalent of a small Walmart] as a distraction when the kids are trying to follow the strange man. According to the narrator, "When someone, even someone who is only six, shouted about an improvised explosive device in a store full of army folk, the result was pure chaos. People screamed and ran and ducked for cover, and the security guard, in what she believed was a show of valor, threw herself on top of Rosie" (190). This is a profoundly unlikely situation, given that most well-trained military children would not dream of calling attention to themselves at the PX, and the security guard would likely be better trained than to "thr[ow] herself" on a six year old. Also, a heavily guarded military base in the United States is extremely unlikely to be the target of an IED, given that all cars are thoroughly searched prior to entry and that the entire compound is fenced.

Despite such unlikely events, this novel does manage to capture some of the uncertainty and anxiety associated with Brat life. One could wonder if the mysterious (and unmilitary) stranger is an embodiment of the unconscious perception of the dangers that reside under the surface of orderly life on the post. Also, the IED incident could represent, metaphorically, the real and ongoing fear the children have that their mother might be injured by such a device when deployed. It seems a shame, though, that these very real concerns are underplayed at the expense of an improbable plot and an unsatisfyingly neat conclusion.

Ashlee Cowles' *Beneath Wandering Stars* (2016) more realistically depicts the fears and losses associated with life as a Military Brat, although the conclusion, which echoes a 19th-century marriage plot, seems rather implausible. In this novel, main character Gabi's brother, Lucas, is injured in Afghanistan, and she decides to walk the *Camino de Santiago* as a way of negotiating with God for his recovery. Eventually she meets up with Lucas's friend and Army buddy Seth, who decides to walk the *Camino* with her, and, unsurprisingly, romance ensues, even though Army Brat Gabi has stated, time and time again, that she has no desire to remain associated with the military after she leaves home.

However, she may be drawn, against her better judgment, toward men like her father, who is the consummate soldier, and to the role she sees her mother playing. Even when her father was not in uniform, Gabi says, he "wore the insignia of the military in the pinched corners of his mouth" (8), and her mother is "charming and perfectly put together—the model military wife…" (17). Gabi knows her place in this clear hierarchy: "When it comes to supporting me or supporting a soldier—no matter how big of a Neanderthal he is—the Army will *always* win" (24). The service member—with his outsized sense of duty to his country—will always come first.

She also knows that moving frequently (and with no permanent destination) is inevitable. She imagines that her family's station wagon is "our galley ship, the open road our Mediterranean Sea. The only thing missing was our Ithaca—the home we were trying to return to despite the detours" (9). This accurately sums up the life of most Military Brats: Dad is first and foremost a soldier, Mom is always perfectly pulled together and supportive, and, as the Brat, Gabi is the last person to be considered as the family moves from place to place with no permanent home in sight.

As Benedis-Grab does in her novel, Cowles emphasizes not only the frequent dislocations but also the drama of military life. Like Benedis-Grab, Cowles describes the ritual of "Retreat": "When the music plays and the flag is lowered, you *stop*. It doesn't matter if you were giving an unconscious person CPR; for forty-five seconds no one moves a muscle" (11). While it is probably not true that CPR would stop as the flag was lowered, Military Brats do feel as if much is riding on their perfect performance of this ritual, this bit of theater. Cowles offers this poignant coda to the event: "A woman leaving the post office slows her stroller, the toddler inside already trained to stay silent" (11). It is worth pausing for a minute to consider a toddler trained to do *anything*, especially keep still and silent for 45 seconds. However, from the moment they become aware of the world outside themselves, Military Brats know the repercussions of not following the rules, even if they do not always know the reasons for following them. Of course, what they are compelled to do becomes transformed into an act of devotion, of patriotism.

The question for Gabi, then, becomes whether she wants to embrace the military life she has always known and replicate it for her children, or whether she wants to strike out on her own, much as she did when she impulsively decided to walk the *Camino*. This heroine's journey is complicated by the fact that Seth has decided to join Gabi on her pilgrimage. Along their journey together, Seth talks to Gabi about his own experiences in the military and as a Brat: "I don't think I could ever live a civilian life after growing up a brat," he says.

## Brat Life

"Some people see needing the military structure as a sign of weakness, but what's the alternative? Working in a cubicle like a dog so you can own a big house in the 'burbs full of crap you don't have time to enjoy? It seems so pointless. Like a merry-go-round of empty promises you get stuck on your entire life" (90). Compared to risking his life for his country, life in the "'burbs" seems "pointless." For Seth, and many other soldiers, life in the military gives him a sense of purpose. As he says, "everyone is working towards the same goal, supporting the same mission" (90). Here, Seth alludes to that longing for a shared sense of purpose, described by Wertsch and others, which draws people toward the military, even when they know the price that their children will pay. However, at the beginning of their journey, and with her brother recuperating in a hospital in Germany as a reminder of the costs of military life, Gabi is not at all sure she wants a military life for herself or her children.

As she considers the pros and cons to a life in the military, Gabi very insightfully outlines the things that are most difficult about life as a Brat. The first is the term "Brat." She recognizes that is a term of endearment, but what bothers her is "being thrown into a club I never asked to join. My dad was the one who signed up for the Army, but the moment the doctor at some hospital with walls the color of lima beans smacked me on the butt and said, 'Welcome to Fort Whatever,' I was in, like it or not." She also hates the "annoying question 'So, where are you from?'" (121). Like Gabi, who eventually learns to respond by saying "pick a place," most Brats in real life come up with a snide shorthand that does not reveal how unpleasant and upsetting moving every few years can be. Sometimes they answer "nowhere" or "everywhere" or just say "my father was in the military," lest people think, as they frequently do, that the primary wage earner in the family has trouble keeping a job. To the outside world, the rigors of Brat life must seem like a choice, like a patriotic duty.

When by herself, though, Gabi admits that she also hates the "constant changes that come with moving so much" (121). Although Gabi's Brat story is not a particularly violent one, it reflects what Wertsch says about the frequent moves, which mean that "by far the most powerful influences on the military child are going to be the

### Three. "Military officers first, and fathers second"

nuclear family and the military lifestyle in which it is caught up. If there are any major problems in that family—alcoholism, abuse of any kind, marital problems, disruptive mental or physical illnesses—the stabilizing influences are again severely diminished" (237). One must depend upon and also please the family members upon whom one is dependent. In fact, "dependent" is the official term for the spouses and children of the service person, and it accurately reflects the strong bonds and the ongoing worry of relying only on one's immediate family for support. Spouses and children are "dependent" on the military member, and on the military, for their survival.

This loyalty translates into a distrust of and even disgust for those not in the world of the military. When a Frenchman criticizes the American military during a night out, Gabi responds with anger: "Maybe it's because I'm part of a miniscule [sic] group of people not in uniform who actually know what it's like—the terror of loss lurking around every corner, the turmoil people like my dad and brother have to wade through as they navigate defending the nation they swore to protect, without losing their souls in the process" (162). Gabi resents this outsider daring to criticize her world, with all its terrors and turmoil. This us-versus-them mentality is common both in soldiers and their dependents. No one can understand patriotism, loyalty, and sacrifice, the argument goes, unless one has served one's country.

As they reach the end of the *Camino*, Seth tells Gabi that she's going to marry a soldier. "It takes a special woman to keep that little platoon in working order," he says. "You've already got the skill set. And the guts" (203). It is a convincing argument: she has been trained all her life to be a military wife, although it is interesting that he does not mention the possibility of her serving in the Army herself. Her family will be her "little platoon," which she will manage with her "skill set" and "guts." Once again, the woman will be the support system at home, while the man goes out to make sacrifices for his family.

Perhaps with this vision in mind, Gabi revises her list of pros and cons of military life, now noting the things that she loves about life as a Brat. Being called a "Brat," she says means that she is "part of an invisible tribe I never asked to join, but … one that will never forsake me" (271). In answer to the "so where are you from?" question, she can now answer that she is "a pilgrim on an endless expedition, a link in a very long chain, a citizen of all lands" (271). Surprises are no longer universally bad, but instead "the surprise of an unexpected journey, the surprise of a stranger's generosity, and the surprise of an answered prayer." Her conclusion is that "people may be the only home the Army issues, but they're the only home that matters" (272). This is a common Brat response: negatives become positives, and problems become challenges to be overcome. Otherwise, the losses would seem too heavy to stand.

By the time the novel ends, Gabi's brother is on the mend, she is considering Seth as a potential husband, and she is seriously considering life as a military wife. She seems to have forgotten the fear and the anger life as a Brat engendered in her. Sure, war causes injury, death, and loss for the families of soldiers, sailors, and airmen, Military Brats are taken from pillar to post (or military post) with no say in where or when they are going, fathers are emotionally distant, and the larger community does not understand; but this is the only life she can imagine, the only life she really wants. Gabi has found the solution for never fitting in, for never belonging anywhere—she has marched back inside the Fortress, this time as a wife and mother to future Brats.

Vicki Bohe-Thackwell's *Too Skinny to Float* (2000) also has a female protagonist, Lanie, who this time is the daughter of the Superintendent of the Air Force Academy. Set in the 1970s during the Vietnam War, the novel centers on Lanie's minor teenage rebellions and their larger real-world motivations and consequences, as does *Beneath Wandering Stars*. As with all Military Brats, and especially with the children of high-ranking officers like Lanie, their conduct is observed and examined for potential harm to the service member, and thereby to the country. Even if their families are falling apart (as Lanie's is), there can be no revealing of the fissures to the world around them.

In Lanie it is possible to see many of the familial stresses identified in earlier chapters of this book. Fourteen-year-old Lanie is both overly parentified and neglected, especially by her mother, who allows her to smoke and who does not notice that Lanie has spirited away a bottle of vodka and goes out in the early morning hours to meet her

## Three. "Military officers first, and fathers second"

boyfriend Peyton. Lanie's father is often away, meeting with various people in Washington about the war. Her mother has "extended spell[s] of melancholy," unalleviated by her never-ending supply of Valium and days spent in bed (10).

Lanie's troubles are exacerbated by finding out that Peyton, whose father has been deployed to Vietnam, will have to move off base, a common experience in Brat life. The service member is still serving his country, but his duty station is Vietnam, where his family cannot follow him (25). Therefore, they are not entitled to base housing during his tour. Like Lanie's mother, Peyton's mom is emotionally challenged by his father's career, having spent time in a mental institution during Peyton's childhood (26). As other writers in this study have noted, life is challenging for those left on the home front, particularly the wives who must pretend, with varying degrees of success, that all is normal inside the Fortress. Throughout the drama of her parents' unfolding marriage, Lanie must remind herself that she is "a general's daughter. Keep up the public image" (35).

However, this façade soon begins to crumble. After she has attempted to shoplift a sweater, as a futile but understandable revenge for her mother's affair, Lanie's father (who has not admitted anything about his marital troubles to his daughter yet) tells her, "'We are not an ordinary family.... We've been called to be leaders, accomplishers'" (49), reminding her that she must lead by example, even if her mother does not. He adds that she is bright and attractive and, until the moment of her misbehavior, he has never been disappointed in her. However, her transgressions (as well as his wife's infidelity) are seen in the military as the officer's fault. "Let's face it," he concludes. "Would you want someone running part of the military whose purpose is to provide protection for this country who can't even control his own family?" (50). The message here is clear, to Lanie and all other Military Brats: the service man is perceived to be a failure as a father and husband, and his potential to lead service men and women into battle is questioned.

To make matters worse, Lanie's father, as a commanding officer, has to make decisions that might help to shorten the war, and if his daughter gets in trouble, he will be too concerned about her to accomplish that vital work. He tells Lanie that his success "'could save so many lives'" (50), but if he is distracted from this mission, "thousands of young American soldiers would be on the battlefield longer because my dad wouldn't be able to do his job" (54). The crime that Lanie has committed—shoplifting--is a common one with teenagers, and one that usually ends with the perpetrator making amends to the store and promising not to do it again. However, given Lanie's situation, her misdeeds could lead to wars being prolonged and lives being lost. Not surprisingly, many Brats evolve all sorts of secretive practices to avoid getting caught, rather than reforming and doing their duty (by being well-behaved) to keep the world safe for democracy.

The domestic and international uncertainties swirling around her have Lanie feeling as if the ground underneath her feet has become unstable. Using a slightly different metaphor, Lanie tells Peyton about trying to teach a nine-year-old cousin to swim. Although she thought that water would always hold someone up, she found that her cousin was "too skinny to float" (56). Lanie has become too deprived of parental support and stability; she is unable to count on the world around her holding her up. The Military Brat often feels "too skinny to float," as if the weight of the world, and of keeping it free, can cause one to sink out of sight.

Lanie does not have the opportunity to save herself and/or redeem herself in her father's eyes by joining the military. Her father never sees that as an option, although he does offer her some oblique advice about being a military wife, which is that "'military life can be hard on a woman. Don't ever marry a military man unless you plan on putting his career first'" (124). Unless she is willing to sacrifice her career and her emotional stability, she should reconcile herself to leaving the military when she turns 18. He also tells her that "personal problems should not interfere" with his life as an Air Force general (64). Consequently, Lanie feels as if her family, like the dream animals she conjures up, is "one of the beautiful little creatures, rotting from the edges out, like bad lettuce" (64). As Wertsch says, military daughters grow up "invisible to their fathers, as ghosts of the Fortress" (111). Lanie's father is aware of her, but usually only when she messes up, and

## Three. "Military officers first, and fathers second"

his only vision of the future for her is the problematic one of becoming a military wife, one that has made her mother miserable.

Lanie comes to feel that her problems do not matter: "Teenage boys were losing their lives fighting a crazy war. All I was losing was my mind. So what if my mother was having an affair and my boyfriend wasn't talking to me and my father was aloof and preoccupied with the war?" (76). She starts to think about when she can move out, marry Peyton, and forget about what her mother had done. "Somehow, though," she says, "neither Nixon's plan for Vietnam nor my plan for my life worked out" (87). Lanie's troubles have been connected to and superseded by the war in Vietnam and her father's mysterious role in mitigating the damages. Eventually, the lies and self-deceptions boil over, with tragic results. Lanie comments that her family was "cloudy and dishonest. We were dishonest because we were all pretending, but I didn't know how to stop it" (128). However, the argument about her mother's infidelity reaches a boiling point, with Lanie's father slapping her mother and her mother, who had been mixing alcohol with Valium, tumbling off their bedroom balcony to her death. After her mother's death, Lanie and her father make a "pact" not to tell anyone about what really happened, which almost seems like normal behavior given the training Lanie has had in keeping family secrets secret.

Although she says that nothing in her life after her mother's death has helped to make her feel better, the novel ends, rather strangely, with Lanie praying that God "fix my mess" (162) and little clue about how that was going to be accomplished. A frame narrative at the beginning of the novel looks ahead to Lanie's future, when she has graduated from college and is going to marry a lawyer. She is "[n]o longer Lanie Julius, daughter of General Julius, superintendent of the Air Force Academy. Now I will be Lanie Ferris [her married name], author and creator of my own life" (ix). However, without the identity of Military Brat, she is "without texture or foothold," and describes herself as "afraid" (xi).

According to Wertsch, "an invisible daughter may be the very essence of assertiveness when it comes to arguing someone *else's* cause, but when the moment comes to put herself on the line on her own behalf, she loses her voice and fades from view" (118). Female

## Brat Life

Brats like Lanie often have more difficulties advocating for themselves. In addition, growing up as a Brat of any gender is "an intensive course in how to discipline one's self to accomplish an objective" (127). Lanie's mission is to help her father slow or stop the loss of lives in the Vietnam War, a task that involves nearly infinite amounts of self-sacrifice. However, as a daughter, she has no models to follow, other than those of military wives; she has no way to redeem herself on the battlefield and see her actions reflected in the eyes of her father. Or, as Wertsch puts it: *"How can a girl-child see her own reflection in a room without mirrors?"* (138, italics in the original). Lanie's choices seem to be between being a dutiful daughter and rebellious teenager, between being military wife and being cast out of the only world she knows.

Like *Too Skinny to Float*, Frances O'Roark Dowell's *Shooting the Moon* (2010) is also about a military daughter during the Vietnam Era. In this novel, 12-year-old Jamie Dexter's brother TJ is in Vietnam. To distract herself from her worry, she begins developing his pictures at the rec center at Ft. Hood, Texas. At first she says she's "combat ready" and "Army through and through" (7), but after speaking with soldiers who have served in Vietnam, she comes to change her mind about the war—and, to a certain extent, about the military mindset she rather mindlessly embraces.

Telling her father the colonel that she's "combat ready" is as familiar to her as "answering the phone 'Colonel Dexter's quarters' or making sure we had our military IDs with us whenever we went to the PX or the commissary [the grocery store on Post] so we could prove who we were, proud citizens of the United States Army" (13). Here, her public identity as a Brat merges with her private sense of self; shopping and even one's home become an extension of life in the military. In particular, Military Brats often think of themselves as citizens of their family's branch of the service, loyal to the United States, but set apart from ordinary citizens by this thoroughgoing commitment to what the Army (or other branches) tells them they need to do for their country. Privileges like subsidized housing and groceries are rewards for such loyalty, and Brats never forget that.

This demand for loyalty is also used to justify the frequent moves, the perpetual uprooting of the family, and the constant threat of war,

## Three. "Military officers first, and fathers second"

which are so familiar to military Brats. Jamie's father would tell her that "the Army way is the right way" when the family headed out once again for "a new destination—Fort Hood, Fort Campbell, Fort Leavenworth." If they feel sad about moving, he reminds them, "'It's about duty, it's about honor, it's about sacrifice.'" In response to this, Jamie tells her readers, "If you weren't an Army brat, that kind of talk would probably have you rolling your eyes. But we believed it. I believed it" (14). After a certain point, most Brats cease to feel (or perhaps cease to recognize that they feel) sad or angry about the frequent moves. After all, it seems petty and selfish to put one's own desires above their country's needs. It's not just that Jamie's family believes; she has internalized that belief.

However, as Jamie ventures outside of her family circle, she interacts with soldiers who have come to question the purpose of the war. For example, when she tells a battle-hardened sergeant that she is "combat ready," he does not respond well: "'Let's call this a combat-free zone, how 'bout it?,'" he says, "Combat-free, duty-free, fancy-free. Land of the free, home of the brave" (43). He spares her the grisly details of war, but his sardonic response about "land of the free, home of the brave" causes her to start asking questions, and she begins to discover that her father is "wrong about a lot" (53). She realizes that her desire to have her brother safe at home results in her losing "good feelings about the war forever. I had lost the excitement that used to get me so wound up I could hardly calm back down again for hours. I lost the green Army men under the shady trees and the thrill I felt when I imagined being an ambulance driver in a combat zone" (117). However, she recognizes that if she loses her faith in the Army she will have "practically lost my own self" (117). To lose faith in the mission is also, for Military Brats, to lose confidence in one's identity, which is forged in dislocation, disruption, and danger in the service of a higher cause.

She finds some consolation when TJ starts sending her pictures of the moon and when she talks her father into keeping a private, whose family has already lost one son, out of the war. She cannot save her brother, though, who ends up in a prisoner-of-war camp for two years. Inspired by TJ, Jamie begins taking pictures herself and hopes, at the end of the novel, that TJ "would look at all the pictures I took of the moon while he was gone, one for every day, even on new-moon days, when the moon hung invisible in the sky, and he would stare at them for almost an hour until he finally said, *You got all the ones I missed"* (163, emphasis in the original).

In this novel, Dowell offers hope that art will help people transition from war back into civilian life and create continuity between those who left and those who stayed at home. However, this does not seem to offer young women much of an option other than trying to boost morale from the home front. Jamie is shooting the moon, literally with her camera, but she is also substituting a camera for a weapon, one that will bring people closer, not destroy them. She is shooting down empty patriotism and raising questions about the personal sacrifices that her culture has led her to believe are necessary and noble.

Roseanne Parry's *Heart of a Shepherd* (2009) features a young adolescent as well, this time a boy, who is left at home while his father goes off to war. Sixth-grader Ignatius, known as Brother, lives on a ranch in Oregon. His father, who is in the Army Reserves, has been ordered to Iraq. During the Iraq and Afghanistan Wars, reserve troops, who usually serve in the States only on weekends and for a few weeks of extended duty each year, were deployed to war zones, often for repeated and extended tours of duty. When Brother asks his father what happens if his men do not want to go to war, his dad replies, "It's our mission, and we'll see it done." He says this in a voice that is "flat and cold, like a person isn't even allowed to think about not going" (9). When the military calls, there is no response but to obey. Brother's mission, whether he likes it or not, is to take care of the ranch while his father is gone.

As his father prepares to deploy, Brother thinks about "the long line of soldiers that have marched away from this table, which is great if you're the patriotic type. But it's not so great if you are the one waiting for your dad to come home" (51). The only options here seem to be being "patriotic" and not complaining when fathers and brothers head off to war or being selfish (and therefore detrimental to the mission). When his friends Paco and Rosita get the news that their parents, who were both deployed, have been injured in Iraq, Brother sees

## Three. "Military officers first, and fathers second"

Paco "make himself stand like a soldier, and I lift up my head and put my shoulders back, but I still feel just as hollow and shy inside" (90).

This portrayal accurately reflects the dilemma faced by sons of male soldiers, according to Wertsch. At first, they find the attention and expectations of the father "thrilling," with "every son of a warrior [being] a kind of crown prince, a child of the correct gender to gain acceptance and affirmation inside the patriarchal world of the Fortress" (142). However, Wertsch says, by adolescence, many sons "have become accustomed to drawing the warrior's eye but not his praise. The warrior father, who for his son represents all warriors, all fathers, does not deliver the overall approval which is vital to his son's self-esteem" (142). Warrior fathers only see sons when they perform as expected, not when they have their own desires and expectations. Loyalty is expected (but not often praised), and individuality is looked on with suspicion.

Thinking about his father in a leadership role in the service, Brother decides that he "couldn't make all those promises. I could never take those salutes and the 'yes, sirs' and then take moms and dads into danger. God knows what I'm supposed to be—not a soldier" (92). For the male Military Brat to resist the father's career is also to reject the father—and, by implication, the country. When Brother's grandfather dies of a heart attack after helping to put out a fire, his dad returns briefly for the funeral, but then he must head back to the war zone. At this point, Brother understands the more humanitarian side of his father's job and the conflicts it raises for him as well. "It is breaking his heart to leave," Brother now knows, "but he'll never rest until they all come home" (155). This change of heart seems to reflect Roberta Trites' version of how adolescents come to accept the reality of death and submit to the societal forces that operate on them. By the end of the novel, Brother has decided that he wants to be a chaplain in the Army. While he does not embrace the ethos of sacrifice entirely, he decides that he, too, has a mission. Like his father, he is willing to subsume his desires into a larger cause. The option of leaving the Fortress now seems impossible.

Sara Lewis Holmes' *Operation YES* (2009) also features a young adolescent boy and confronts the realities of deployment. Main character Bo, the son of an Air Force base commander, finds himself in the classroom of sixth-grade teacher Miss Loupe, who specializes in teaching dramatic improvisation. During his year with Miss Loupe, Bo's brother, who is serving in Afghanistan, is wounded. To complicate things further, his cousin Geri is also staying with them while her mother is deployed as a nurse in Iraq, and these children are surrounded by the fears and stresses of multiple deployments. With the support of their teacher, the kids come up with a plan to sell plastic army men to raise money for wounded soldiers at Walter Reed National Military Medical Center. This is the "Operation YES" of the title.

The novel is less about the operation than it is about the challenges of Bo's life as a Military Brat. In six years, Bo has moved five times, and as the family settle into their new quarters, he wonders "how many houses from now he would be thinking back to this room, to this house, to this town, and know that everyone here had mostly forgotten who Bo Whaley was. It was eerie, like thinking about himself in a long hall of mirrors, each one smaller than the last" (46). Military housing on one base mimics military housing on every other base, and Brats know that their presence in each house is temporary, as it is for all the others who have lived there before. As Truscott puts it, military quarters are "stage sets, scenic backdrops" (27) in which various families drop in and shortly move out, and Wertsch reflects Bo's feeling that "it is like living in a hall of mirrors, where the Fortress, the warrior, and the family all reflect one another endlessly" (27). Inevitably, Bo and other Brats come to feel as if the lives that they are living aren't just temporary, but also unreal. He wonders how his mother does it: "Start over and over, each time they moved? Didn't she mind being ripped up?" (105). Of course, the role of the military spouse is somewhat different than that of the Brat. The spouse may have an emotional foundation based on having a stable home throughout childhood. The Brat, on the other hand, never knows when he or she will be "ripped up."

When Bo is told his dad may command a wing (a large group of planes and their pilots) in Afghanistan, "the dead center of Bo's chest tightened," and he thinks about a glass case in the school library that

### Three. "Military officers first, and fathers second"

contains the pictures of soldiers killed in combat (105). Also, if his father is deployed, the rest of the family would have to move off base. "Where did you go if the Air Force didn't tell you where you had to go?" he wonders (106). Significantly, Bo's house key is attached to a REMOVE BEFORE FLIGHT tag from the planes his father has flown, and he rips the tag off in frustration over not knowing where his family will live next year. He points out that his father has chosen to do what the Air Force tells him to do, and Bo has not. "Fine. Who cares where I live?" he says. "Who cares what I want to do? Who cares if the only thing that gets REMOVED is *me*?" (155, emphasis in the original). For Bo, as for all military Brats, there is no choice; there is no flight, no transcendent performance of duty, only removal, like garbage.

Toward the end of the novel, Bo and his cousin walk through the base, giving a vivid and accurate description of life inside the Fortress, as they walk "past the curved domes of concrete hangars and the massive new brick-and-glass fire station and the well-lit base gym and the now-closed BX and the smaller shopette with video rental and a ten-pump gas station ... past signs advertising Sunday brunch at the Officer's Club and bingo at the NCO Club ... past the sweep of the chapel roof and through the maze of enlisted housing and into the officers' section. They walked past house after house, down the streets named after states ... after generals ... after aircraft" (165–166). Every Navy and Air Force base, and every post for Army Brats, looks like this: the mundane (but orderly) trappings of family life; the gym, stores, and bingo at the NCO club. Most of these things, however, serve to distract the dependents from the reality of war, although the street names, airfields, tanks, and ships at the margins remind them of the ultimate mission. This is a community that at any minute is prepared to send its service men and women into battle, while it keeps the dependents distracted by brunch, swimming pools, and movie theaters.

At the novel's close, Bo and his family are leaving for Korea, where his father is going to work at the Combined Air Operations Center, and Geri is headed back to Seattle, where her mom will join her. Families are reunited, and Bo does not have to face the difficulties presented by a wartime deployment and the resulting separation of the family. In spite of the turmoil he has been through, Bo happily heads off to a new posting. He removes the tags that link him to the world, to personal desires, and he is ready to take off once again. He is no longer rejecting the values of the dangerous and demanding military world around him; he is embracing them. After all, he has very little choice—as long as he is a child.

Although it is set in an earlier time than the other novels, Michael Joseph Lyons' *BRAT and the Kids of Warriors* (2017) is perhaps the most ruthless in its depiction of the toll that life as a Brat takes on the "kids of warriors." In this novel, Jack, Rabbit (Kirsten), and Queenie (Laura) McMasters are on their way to Germany in 1957 as part of the U.S. occupying force after World War II. Their father is a Lieutenant Colonel in the 4th Armored Division, and he has arrived before them. As they board the USS *Upshur*, a Naval ship on the way to Germany, Jack tells his siblings, "We should enjoy this ship while we can. Once we're there, we're right back to square one—with nothing. Our friends are gone. Everything and everyone we know is gone. We don't know a thing about the place we're headed. We don't know where we'll live or when we'll go to school, or what that will be like. Except for Mom and Dad, we won't know a single soul. Who knows if we'll even make friends?" (10). This is the dilemma of the Military Brat: the only constant in your life is your family; the rest is uncertain, so you might as well have fun in the meantime.

Jack copes with this uncertainty in the time-honored way of Military Brats: he hides what he really feels and gives the adults around him the face they want to see: "Jack just naturally understood that if you give people what they want or at least whey they expect they can have, you tended to stay out of trouble" (8). From early on, Jack, like most Brats, has learned to please the adults around him, mostly because the price of not appearing to comply can be devastating. To stay in the "good graces" of the adults that surround him means that he will not be in danger of embarrassing his father (and incurring his wrath), and, most importantly, of endangering the mission.

Jack's mother is onboard, literally and figuratively, running her little "platoon" while they travel to meet his father. Everything Jack's mother says to the children "was covered under her motto: 'Look

## Three. "Military officers first, and fathers second"

sharp, act sharp, be sharp'" (21). The key is to appear in control, loyal, and presentable. As Wertsch says, the military wife and mother "holds the position of official interpreter for the family, licensed to translate the words and actions of father or child into language the other can understand. And since she is the one and only interpreter, her reports are vested with absolute credibility; she can color them as she pleases, to suit her purpose, subtly altering the way one party sees the other" (85). Their mother's mantra is drawn from the protocols of the military, but she also puts her spin on the commands, channeling their father and the military in ways the children can understand and with which they are able to comply. The kids may not be able to serve in the military yet, but they can "look sharp, act sharp, be sharp." They also assume that this is what their father wants, since their mother has told them that it is.

Part of looking sharp means respecting the chain of command, which also applies to children. Even though Jack and his siblings are children travelling to the same place as other Brats, they are admonished not to play with children whose parents are of a different rank: "It was the old rule that officers' kids can't play with sergeants' kids, and they can't play with us" (62). Wertsch says that these segregations by rank create "a world with an entirely different dynamic from that of civilian America. The assumption underlying military life is not to affirm and equalize ... but to maintain the most rigid hierarchy possible, built around dominance and subordination and emphasizing class stratification in every way. For the military—and military in any country—this is absolutely critical to the life and purpose of the organization" (286). This hierarchy reminds Brats that there is no separation between the life of the service members and the lives of their dependents. The kids, however, find a characteristically Brat way to solve this problem; they appear to conform while violating the rule in private. Jack says "As usual, you followed standard operating procedure. Ignore the rule till you get busted" (62). Brat sneakiness, he adds, is a "fine art form" (74). When one has no autonomy, even when playing with other children, one learns to lie, and to lie well.

In addition to learning early to lie in order to have some agency in life, Military Brats quickly become aware that they are expected to act as representatives of their country. Commander Allen, who is on board the ship with the siblings and other Brats, tells them that "whatever you do here in Germany, you are not just a bunch of kids running around. Listen to me closely. Always remember you represent the United States Military and, most importantly, the United States of America. That matters. Represent your country well. You will meet many people, and not just Germans, but people from all over Europe. Never forget you symbolize the best of America." The kids respond with a pro forma "yes, sir," but Jack also means what he says, at least in part, "because he knew he represented America" (87–88). This is a delicate balance: one is aware of putting on a show, but after a while, one also internalizes the lesson and attaches value to it. One does not just play at being an ambassador; one becomes one.

When they arrive, the kids begin to acclimate as part of the occupation force in Germany after the war. Not long after, though, Jack begins to get in trouble with his father, who is, much like Pat Conroy's difficult father, "a challenge, and often intimidating. But sometimes he was also amazing" (95). Although his mother warns him that he *"had better not do anything to upset your father"* (104, italics in the original), Jack transgresses by yawning dramatically in church. After the service, as they are headed home, his father's response is instantaneous, "growl[ing]" to his son immediately after they leave the church: "You sorry excuse for a human being. You are one extremely poor representative of the United States of America. Every self-respecting German in that place saw your slothful, bored, lazy demeanor" (152). Jack's father speaks to him as he would to a green recruit, calling him "a sorry excuse for a human being" and a "poor representative of the United States of America." He also places the eyes of "every self-respecting German" on his son, who has done nothing more than yawn in church. For this relatively minor transgression, Jack is not just worried about being admonished but also about being physically assaulted, "going the rounds" with his father, and he prays to get out of the car as fast as possible. Eventually the tension lessens, and "whenever the colonel's tension eased, the whole family's tension eased" (153). Although his father calms down, his insults and threats remain in Jack's mind, making him even more determined not to get caught in the future.

### Three. "Military officers first, and fathers second"

However, shortly after this incident, several kids do get caught fighting. When confronted about their behavior, "every kid stood tall, though their faces had the thousand-yard stare of a shell-shocked soldier" (187). They all know, as Jack does, that if "your actions bring negative attention to the colonel, you're in deep trouble. Right, wrong, or indifferent, you are going to get it. The rules are clear: You never, *never* make a military officer look bad. You do it, and it can affect that officer's career." These thoughts fill Jack with "dread" (188). This dread is warranted, and as Jack ran up the stairs of the family quarters, his father caught him and "slapped him a hard one upside the back of his head. Jack went down hard" (189), and his nose started to bleed. It is important to keep in mind here that these are not soldiers; these are children who have become "shell-shocked soldier[s]" who live in fear of their fathers' wrath.

Eventually, his mother brings him ice, runs a bath, and gets him clean clothes. She "didn't show anger, nor did she show sympathy. She didn't show anything at all" (190). This is the typical response of the military spouse: loyalty to the service member is paramount, even when it comes to abuse. When Jack tries to explain that it was not his fault, his mother says, "Jack, who started it doesn't matter. What matters is that you made your father look bad. You kids simply can't afford to make your father look bad. Do you understand that? Do you understand why?" (191). The answer is that inside the Fortress, kids are not allowed to be kids, as the consequences for misbehavior may well lead to war (or at least that is what they are led to believe). Therefore, it "doesn't matter" that his father, a grown man and a battle-hardened soldier, is harming her son.

Some of the other children who were caught fighting were treated even more violently than Jack was. Kevin, who was involved in the fight, comes to school the next day, and his "face was swollen and dark." Jack "realized how Kevin got it, and guilt flooded him" (195). Jack feels guilty that he contributed to events that resulted in Kevin being hurt, and he is embarrassed that his punishment was comparatively light. As the kids self-defensively joke about their punishments, Jack thinks, "*We weathered this one, but I need to do better at keeping these guys safe*" (198, italics in the original). As Pat Conroy describes life with his violent father: "When my father was off killing the enemy, his family slept securely, and not because he was making the world safe for democracy" ("Introduction" xix). Not surprisingly, the man trained to protect the country by destroying the enemy can become a violent and dangerous force in his family, one who makes the world safer but who makes his family feel unsafe.

The ambivalence that Jack feels in relation to his father is common to the sons of service men. As Wertsch says, "At the outset, the sons of warriors bask in the glow of their fathers' reflected glory, the cumulative glory of the ages which resides in the person of every warrior, whether or not he has been tested in battle. The soldier-hero is not a storybook abstraction for the sons of warriors. He is an active, powerful, compelling presence, at once challenging and exhilarating, part of a continuum of brave and bold warriors going back to the beginning of history" (144). The soldier/father is both larger than life and very much a real (and sometimes dangerous) presence in the household. There is reflected glory, but there is also an ever-present threat. In addition, if the son fails to live up to the promise his father expects of him, the possibility of banishment looms. This is what Wertsch describes as the "terrible dilemma for many a son of the Fortress ... that he is *supposed* to be bred for the exalted company of warriors," but if he slips or is ignored by that father, "he is abandoned to the world of the mother" (190). A boy who fails to live up to his father's standard is banished to the humiliating world of women. As Jack's mother shows, however, even if a son wanted to be comforted by his mother, a soldier's wife rarely offers her child a soft place to land.

Family violence is not the only fallout of life in the military; so is the psychological debilitation of military wives. Jack's friend Kevin's mother provides an excellent example. When the boys arrive at Kevin's house, his mother is "seated in an old, overstuffed chair in a far corner. She seemed slightly heavyset and strangely removed. Remaining perfectly still, she was like a female Buddha sitting there in the dark" (205). The tranquil and removed Buddha is quickly replaced by the reality of a frantic, alcoholic mother. Having a meltdown about Kevin's dirty shoes, she starts drinking even more heavily and blaming Kevin for her drinking. As a result, Kevin's dad hits him in the face,

### Three. "Military officers first, and fathers second"

again. Kevin's carelessness with his shoes, and not his mother's alcoholism or his father's violence, is at fault.

The next day Kevin downplays the incident: "Let's just say my mom was kinda ticked off about it. And when she gets upset, the colonel gets upset. And when you're the son who caused this tragedy, the colonel concludes you're an ass-wipe. But you know *that* drill" (272). They all do know the drill: a misbehaving son leads to an unhappy mother, which leads to a disapproving and violent father. Kevin cannot talk seriously to his friends about the violence in his home and has long ago "promised himself he'd never tell anyone about his mom's drinking. It was just something he couldn't reveal. So once again he resisted his need to talk about it—even to Jack" (272). As Truscott says, "Military families keep closed ranks; they mind their own business ... life on a post is often compared to life in a goldfish bowl. Any hint of family problems, even in casual conversation, could have an impact on a family's reputation, and ultimately, on a father's career" (4). Talking openly about a mother's drinking or a father's beatings in the goldfish bowl of a military base would lead to disaster—for the child and, perhaps, for the world. If things are not already bad enough, if Kevin were to complain outside the family, things might get much worse. His father might face punishment for not correctly disciplining his children (and his wife), and the violence and drinking at home would likely escalate. In addition, the stakes are high during this time: the U.S. is in a Cold War with Russia, and Germany is the "battlefield." Family discord, which could affect unit cohesion, conceivably, could lead to World War III. This sounds melodramatic, but it was—and is—part of the military mindset and part of the lives of Brats.

Toward the end of the novel, the kids are ordered (literally, not figuratively) to have lunch with some German children as part of the Army's military/civilian outreach. The American children tell the German kids, "We were ordered to play with you. But I didn't even remember that. We're used to getting orders that we have to obey instantly. For us, if you don't obey, they will kill you. Well, not exactly kill you, but you know what I mean. Our fathers are military officers first, and fathers second" (306). Kevin responds playfully "or third," and another girl chimes in with "or fourth," and their response to this clear

## Brat Life

hierarchy that places military children on the very bottom causes all the children to laugh (306). Clearly, they realize they have little choice but to laugh. To allow themselves to be upset by the ways in which they are devalued would be devastating.

While this novel uncovers some of the challenges and even the horrors of Brat life, its lighthearted tone undercuts much of the critique, as is the case with several of the novels discussed in this chapter. The novel falls back on some of the clichés of the Brat experience: making do, being resilient, following orders in public and disobeying them in private, and downplaying the violence at home. Still, by at least acknowledging these issues as potential problems, *BRAT* does open a channel for further conversation about them.

These seven novels cover five decades of Military Brat life, and they explore deployment, injury, death, moving, necessary deceptions, and the ordinary incongruities and confusions of childhood. These fictional children, like their Brat counterparts in real life, live around warriors, play on model (and sometimes real) tanks and aircraft, and accustom themselves early on to the rituals of the theater that is life on post or base. They learn that they must represent their countries and their fathers' (and sometimes their mothers') leadership skills, and they learn to cope with having no permanent residence or lifetime friends. These works are a welcome addition to young adult literature and represent a hitherto hidden aspect of childhood inside the Fortress. The usually imaginary scourges of childhood and young adulthood—witches and trolls, post-apocalyptic wastelands, vampire lovers—are replaced by the real-life specters of family violence, nuclear annihilation, or the absence or loss of loved ones. The military base is Foucault's panopticon on a massive scale: observation is omnipresent, judgment is internalized, and one's actions have consequences far beyond losing one's cell phone for a week. These novels show civilian children a hitherto unavailable glimpse into the lives of classmates, neighbors, and friends.

Most importantly, though, these novels let children in the military know that they are not alone, that they form part of Long Gray Line of children who have been carted from pillar to military post, who have told themselves that they like the adventure of military life,

### Three. "Military officers first, and fathers second"

and who have had to internalize the near-constant anxiety they feel about their military parents. Hopefully they will open the eyes of those inside and outside of the military to the needs of these children, who, regardless of their own wishes, have found themselves trapped inside the Fortress. These books do not downplay the rigors and the terrors of military life, but they do let military children know that their conflicting feelings—of love and fear, of patriotism and anger, of the need to be seen and the need to dissemble—are shared by others. They may often feel alone, cocooned in that family car headed away from friends and familiar locations, but there are many others who have travelled that nighttime highway (complete with jaw-clenching father driving) along with them.

# Four

# "Military brats don't have hometowns"
## *Adult Novels About Brat Life*

> I was living in Massachusetts, sitting at my desk one day writing a nonfiction snippet about how it felt to move so often, about what it was like being an army brat. That little section, which is in the novel, was so full of feeling for me. I knew there was a lot of material to be mined.
> —Elizabeth Berg, from the Reader's Guide to *Durable Goods*, 196

Like the novels for young adults discussed in the previous chapter, these stories of life inside the Fortress chronicle the experiences of children in the military: the frequent moves, the violent fathers and protective or emotionally-absent mothers, the familiarity of life on U.S. military bases throughout the world, the pride in one's father and in one's country, and the near-constant fear that something will happen to the parent whose mission is holding the entire family together. However, unlike fiction directed toward adolescents, these adult novels take an even closer look at family dysfunction, at the strangeness of life inside the Fortress, and at the outside forces that impinge upon these military families specifically and the military in general.

To do this, these works take an unsparing look at the rigidity, the aggression, and the distance—physical and emotional—of the fathers and their effects on their wives and children. They refuse to take easy

## Four. "Military brats don't have hometowns"

refuge in patriotism or the vaunted resilience of Military Brats and instead focus on the often absurd and frequently traumatic aspects of Brat life. Pat Conroy's *The Great Santini* (1976); Bobbie Ann Mason's *In Country* (1985); Elizabeth Berg's trilogy *Durable Goods* (1995), *Joy School* (1997), and *True to Form* (2002); and Sarah Bird's *The Yokota Officers Club* (2001) look at time periods just before and after the Vietnam War and place the children at the center of the novels set in Okinawa, Japan, South Carolina, and Texas. The experiences of these protagonists have many of the hallmarks of Brat life, especially of white children growing up as dependents of military officers, and they also show how these experiences are shaped by the gender of the protagonists.

Perhaps the most well-known of the Brat novels, Pat Conroy's *The Great Santini*, is in equal parts horrifying and poignant. Based on his own family's experiences living with his Marine fighter pilot father, the novel charts the family's move to their final posting in Beaufort, South Carolina, next to the Parris Island Marine Base where their father is to be stationed. The main character, Ben, who is based closely on Conroy, and his family settle into a large, old house in Beaufort, where they try to make a new home and stay out of the way of their larger-than-life father. As Catherine Seltzer puts it in *Understanding Pat Conroy*, "*The Great Santini* engages in a complicated consideration of a broader form of paternalistic power, tracing in particular the ways that institutionalized constructions of masculinity shape identity, often warping it to the point of alienation" (29). This novel, however, is not just about "paternalistic power"; it is about how the military both warps and validates that power.

The story begins with Ben, his mother, and his siblings waiting for their father to fly in to meet them. "He had lost count how many times he had waited beside landing strips," the narrator says about Ben, "scanning the sky for the approach of his father, his tall, jacketed father, to drop out of the sky, descending into the sight of his waiting family, a family who over the long years had developed patient eyes, sky-filled eyes, wing-blessed eyes" (11). Imagine the power of such a moment: your "tall, jacketed" father drops down in a fighter jet, descending from the heavens like a deity, and strides down the runway

## Brat Life

in uniform to meet his family. The hero arrives, and the family, blessed by his arrival, quickly begins planning its next moves, anticipating the changes—mostly negative—that their father's arrival will bring. As Seltzer says, "In wartime the battles in which marines are engaged are clear; out of the field, however, they must invent new ways of testing their skill and bravado, often devising contests that cross into the world of the absurd, offensive, and dangerous" (29–30). There is no question that Bull Meecham's life on the ground is "absurd, offensive and dangerous," especially to his wife and children, who are expected to prove their loyalty and obedience through a series of bizarre contests and violent outbursts.

These tests are often inflicted on Ben's mother, Lillian, who has to adjust to having her authoritarian husband back home when she has been running the show during his absence. "It was a universal law in military families that mothers could not maintain the strict discipline enforced by fathers to whom discipline was a religion and a way of life," the narrator comments. "When the military man left for a year, the whole family relaxed in a collective, yet unvoiced sigh. For a year, there was a looseness, a freedom from tension, a time when martial law was suspended. Though a manless house was an uncompleted home, and though the father was keenly missed, there was a laxity and fragile vigor that could not survive his homecoming" (17). This "looseness" and "fragile vigor" dissipates immediately upon Bull's arrival. Almost as soon as their father's plane touches down, the Meecham children's mother "would hand the household over to her husband without a single word passing between them" (18). While this transition may appear seamless, it is fraught with a toxic mix of fear and resentment on Lillian's part.

This man, to whom "command" over the family has been returned, however, is an enigma to his children. Ben's sister Mary Anne tells him that Bull Meecham is "hard to figure out. He loves his family, more than anything in the world except the Marine Corps, yet none of us ever have a real conversation with him" (19). The military father is often unknowable to his children; he has trained himself to master and conceal his emotions, his weaknesses, to be a better Marine (or soldier, airman, or sailor). Revealing conversations with

## Four. "Military brats don't have hometowns"

one's children is not part of that discipline. Yet it is this father upon whom the family is dependent, emotionally and practically.

Part of this submission to the order of the father is acquiescence to the frequent moving required by military life. Ben comments that his family were "middle class migrants, and all of them were part of a profession whose most severe punishment was rootlessness and whose sweetest gift was a freedom granted by highways and a vision of America where nothing was permanent and everything possible" (25). This encapsulates both the pressures and the pleasures of frequent moves. Rootlessness, according to Ben, is a gift but also the "most severe punishment" that can be inflicted on young children. For example, one of Ben's sisters talks to another about friends left behind at other bases. "They're as good as dead," she says, sardonically. "But don't worry, you'll make lots of new friends in this town we're moving to. Wonderful friends. Then Dad will get orders again and they'll all be dead too" (14). This is the push and pull of military life: Brats make friends rapidly and they let go of them equally quickly. The past is always dead for the Brat.

Although the Meecham family members are pawns on a chess game being played by generals, they are also bound together by their rootlessness and by a freedom that comes from having no ties that bind. Ben sees this situation as one that extends to all U.S. Military families: "Movement, travel, impermanence, and passing in the night were laws of the tribe.... They pack, move, unpack, burrow in, and nervously await their next orders. When summers come a moving fever hits many of them, even when the orders command that they stay where they are" (29–30). Each new base represents "counterfeit security" for a few years, but the law of military life demands that military children both believe in that security and love the adventure of leaving. In fact, this cycle of moving is so ingrained in Brats' psyches that they long to move even when the military tells them to stay put—or even when they age out of Bratdom. A "moving fever" can take over even when they have long been part of civilian life.

Although military bases provide a kind of temporary security, Ben says that he can find no connection to the various bases on which he has lived: "Every house was a temporary watering place where warriors gathered for training and the perfection of their grim art before the tents were struck again" (44). Every house is temporary, "washed out," a backdrop to the father's mission; there are no "imperishable allegiances," no "fealty" to one place or another. Ben longs for "a sense of place, of belonging, and of permanence. He wanted to live in one house, grow old in one neighborhood, and wanted friends whose faces did not change yearly" (44). Interestingly, Conroy himself eventually settled in Beaufort, which he calls Ravenel in the book, where he lived until the end of his life. He did "grow old in one neighborhood," even if he arrived at the neighborhood initially as part of a nomadic tribe of military families.

With the bravado common to many in the military, Bull tells his kids that they "are lucky to be part of a Marine Corps family. There are no kids in America as well trained in geography as you. You've been to more places than civilian kids even know about. Travel is the best education in the world" (46). Most Brats have been told this—or something very much like it—in their childhoods, especially if they complain (and many do not) about moving frequently and having to leave school and friends behind. Brats are told that they know more about the world than their civilian counterparts and therefore are better educated. Bull's kids sarcastically respond that they are "lucky" that they "get to go to four high schools instead of just one" (47) and that they are "lucky enough to be absolutely friendless through an entire school year until the month of May. Then I make lots of new friends. Then I'm lucky enough to have Daddy come home with a new set of orders. Then I'm lucky enough to move in the summer and lucky enough to be absolutely friendless when school starts back in the fall" (47). Some luck, indeed, to have no friends at the beginning of almost every school year and to know that there is absolutely nothing one can do about it—except to stop caring about making friends.

As the kids look for anything that might help them begin to feel at home in Ravenel, they hear a jet passing overhead. This is "a sound familiar to all of them, its thunder rumbling across them as though they were long sheets of glass. It was a legitimate sound of home, one that would remind the Meecham children of their youth more strongly than the singing bells of ice cream trucks or the cadences of lullabies"

## Four. "Military brats don't have hometowns"

(49). It may be difficult for civilian children to understand this phenomenon, but to Military Brats, the trappings of war—the fighter jets, the tanks, the submarines, the war ships—are as familiar to them as ice cream trucks and lullabies are to civilian kids. These signs of war, of killing, become the "legitimate sound of home." Military Brats are the "long sheets of glass" whose sole job is to reflect the values of the violent world in which they have found themselves.

As they settle into their new home, Bull reminds his children that they are "Marine kids and can chew nails while other kids are sucking on cotton candy. Marine kids are so far ahead of other kids that it's criminal. Why? Because of discipline" (59). This discipline that sets them apart from cotton-candy-sucking civilian children is necessary in the face of the disruptions in their lives—both of moving every few years and of living with an angry and unpredictable father and a mother who enables his violent behavior. Most civilian children see their Brat counterparts as intruders, strangers, oddballs who never seem to have quite the right clothing and who often disappear with little fanfare; they never notice the discipline and terror that underscore their lives. Military fathers are often oblivious to this conflict, though. As Ben puts it, "It is often difficult for military officers to grasp the fact that the civilian world does not hold them in shivering awe" (60). A Marine Corps pilot, or an Army colonel, or a Navy commander cannot fathom the indifference—and sometimes outright hostility—that the civilian world has for those in the military, but they can demand that awe and obedience from their children.

As this dutiful family starts to unpack, Ben catalogues the "accoutrements" of every military home, which includes "four statues of Buddha in various postures and degrees of corpulence ... five sets of brass candlesticks from Taiwan, a large painting of a Seine river scene which Bull had bought while drunk in Paris ... embroidered blankets from Arabia, Libyan tapestries, and swords from Toledo crossed over a coat of arms" (65–66). These are the trappings of a life spent abroad, in the various places occupied by the American military: Europe, the Middle East, and most of Asia. They represent plunder as well as treasure and are signs and symbols of occupation and dominance of lands and peoples. They are trophies, but they are also the only signs for Military

## Brat Life

Brats of continuity and collective memory—the only part of home that is permanent (unless the movers misplace or destroy them).

As Ben considers his once-again new school, he realizes that as soon as he "was awash with the beneficent realization that he was a stranger no longer, that he belonged almost as much as anyone else, it was then that the Marine would come home with orders and announce that the family would move again that June" (151). Belonging, for the Military Brat, is always a temporary feeling. To cope with this transitoriness, Ben has become "a prodigy of the first impression," especially around adults. "So often had Ben been drilled in the proper manner in which to greet Marines and their wives that his act was no longer an act but an intrinsic manifestation of his personality" (181). Brats come to embrace what has been drilled into them since infancy: they are always polite, always on display, always ready to do their families proud (or to hide anything that might bring shame upon them). This is reflected in all the fictional and nonfictional accounts of Brat life presented in this book. Brats learn to appear to be whatever others want them to be to avoid incurring the wrath of their fathers (and mothers) and thereby disgracing their country.

In *The Pat Conroy Cookbook*, Conroy has this to say about this longing for home, which he says "was a powerful as fire in my bloodstream. I lived at twenty-three different addresses as my father moved from base to base flying the warplanes that kept our nation's airways safe. When asked where my hometown was, I answered in a complete silence that baffled strangers and embarrassed me" (475). There is much in this passage that is typical of Brat life—the longing for home, the silence in the face of unanswerable questions, the sense of insignificance and dependence. Many Brats learn to guard against those "soft places" and refuse to acknowledge the need for a permanent home, telling themselves that they are too tough, too resilient, too adaptable, or even too worldly-wise, to need a place to belong. Mostly, this is a defense against the "baffled strangers" and their inevitable pity for a childhood that looks to them vagabond and rootless.

In addition to longing for permanence and security, Ben and his family are living with chaos and violence inside the household. In one memorable scene, Ben challenges his father to a basketball game, a

## Four. "Military brats don't have hometowns"

version of which they have played (and Bull always won) for years. This time, Ben defeats his father, who initially changes the rules after Ben's win, demanding another chance to beat his son. Lillian intervenes, but this only fires up Bull's temper, and he viciously kicks his wife, and then follows Ben into the house, bouncing the basketball off his head as he ascends the stairs. In addition to the physical pain, Ben's victory is undercut by his awareness that he will "have the night to consider all the symbols of this long march: the heads of sons, the pride of fathers, victors, losers, the faces of kicked wives, the fear of families, the Saturdays in the reign of Santini" (132). He will never escape his father's rage and his mother's pain. At the end of this violent and humiliating encounter, Bull adds a final insult, calling Ben his "favorite daughter" (132), and Ben proudly throws the intended slur back on him, saying that "this little girl just whipped you good" (132). In this incident, Ben has recognized that being a "little girl" is only insulting to Bull, not to him; the key to defeating The Great Santini is being impervious—as his father is not—to diminishment of his manhood.

However, it is more complicated than that. Bull is not just a force of chaos and violence; he is, in many ways, transcendent—and terrifying. Although Ben sees his father and his comrades in arms as "having just come down from doing things that smaller, punier men could never do, doing things only gods could do" (202), he recognizes that this can also have a cost for the children of those "gods." Larger men such as these Marine Corps pilots are, like gods, forgiven their minor (and sometimes even major) transgressions. Lillian warns Ben that "the ego is bloated into something monstrous when a man decides to make the Marine Corps a career" (213). A Marine Corps pilot is even more monstrous when he is not "doing things that smaller, punier men could never do" and is instead trying to be a parent. For example, when Lillian asks Bull if it bothers him that his children are afraid of him, he responds, "Hell no ... it would bother me if they weren't afraid of me. It's my job to see that they stay afraid of me" (238). Here, Bull seems to be transferring his fighting spirit to the family dynamic and assuming that what applies to the Marines who serve under him should apply to his children as well. Fear leads to obedience, and, in the context of war, it results in

## Brat Life

everyone coming home alive, while fear in a family leads to alienation between parent and child.

Along with this fear, "Bull wanted to pass on the gift of fury to his oldest son, a passion to inflict defeat on others, even humiliation" (280). Bull wants his children—especially his male children—to be furious AND afraid. Seltzer summarizes the situation this way: "For Ben this classic Oedipal dilemma plays out with a fresh sense of urgency; as graduation nears along with its inevitable conferral of adulthood, Ben must not only come to terms with the complicated dynamic of his own home, but must also decide if he will replicate—and thus tacitly accept—a model of manhood that he claims to abhor by joining the Marine Corps as his parents expect him to do" (30). As a boy about to become a capital "M" Man, Ben has the prototypical male Brat dilemma: should he join the military as his father wants him to do, and thereby "replicate ... a model of manhood he claims to abhor," or will he struggle, without any role models, to create a new version of masculinity, one that began to emerge when he challenged his father's insults to his manhood.

The situation is even more fraught for Ben's sister Mary Ann, who is furious but silent for most of the novel. As Seltzer says, Mary Ann "is often reduced to a form of communication that only she and Ben, her chief confidante, can understand" (43). She becomes "a largely silenced figure, one doomed to speak in dead languages or to shout into a vacuum" (44). This is due to the dilemma Wertsch outlines in her book that daughters of warriors face. She cannot be, like Ben, a favored son destined to follow in his father's footsteps, and, if she does not want to adhere to traditional gender codes and, preferably, marry a military man, her father has no interest in her. Unlike her genteel, Southern mother, Mary Ann, Seltzer says, "insists upon a fierce, if irreverent, form of autonomy, and as a result she finds herself alienated in a culture that has no meaningful way of accommodating her voice" (44). While Ben can both physically and verbally defeat her father, Mary Ann has no recourse but in silence.

This rage and accumulated tension reach their apotheosis after a particularly dramatic drunken Mess Night, a formal dinner celebrating Marine *esprit de corps*, when Bull comes home ready to inflict

## Four. "Military brats don't have hometowns"

violence on his family, particularly his wife. As Ben hears him arrive, he knows "this would be one of the bad times. He girded himself and knew this would be a conflict that would extend the thresholds of his fear of his father and his cowardice before the plowman who had granted him life. He would act bravely; he would force himself to act bravely. But he knew. Even brave acts could not allay the fear: the consuming fear that rules him whenever he had to face Bull Meecham boy to man" (426). Ben sees that "the dragon is loose" in his father's eyes and that he is destined to challenge him, "bound by the rites of a perverted chivalry written into the family's history" (427). However, this time, Ben realizes that he has been growing stronger. At the end of this battle, Bull gives up, and Ben has a chance to hit him but finds "he could not hit the face of the father that would be the face of his father for all time" (428). After this flight, Bull staggers out into the night and passes out in a field. Ben must bring him home. As Bull shrugs off his help, calling him "Mama's boy," Ben responds by telling his father, over and over, that he loves him. Although his father's response is to run away, Ben is "smiling, exhilarated, liberated and meanly enjoying a weapon he did not know lay in his arsenal" (431). Expressing love, Ben has discovered, is more effective than violence or fear.

Even though this encounter with his father has given him some insights, Ben laments to his mother, "I don't know anyone's history, not even my own" (438). One wonders if this is, in part, why Conroy wrote this novel: to understand his father, his mother, his siblings, and himself. The lack of a coherent life narrative is also common to the Brat experience. Chronicling important moments means remembering first where you were living, then whether your military parent was home or abroad, and finally, whether you were in the process of moving or settling in. There are no home bases (although there are plenty of bases) and consequently no anchoring experience, other than frequent disruptions, on which to build a story. Finally, there is only, for Pat Conroy and many other male Brats, the conflict with the father.

The novel ends with the crash of Bull's plane and his death, although in real life, Conroy's father lived past his time in the Marines, and his parents eventually divorced. In the book, Lillian is prepared for the crash, as all military wives prepare for the possible death of their husbands: "There was a strength derived from living with the possibility of disaster and it was a source of energy that could be used when it had to be. Like her husband, she had her duties" (456). This strength carries her through her husband's sudden but not entirely unexpected death, through the funeral, and through her family's separation from the military. A side note: most civilians do not realize that military families surrender their connections to military bases upon the death of the serving spouse, often being forced to leave base housing soon after the service member's death. The life they have known for decades is over in an instant. In Ben's family's case, they leave Ravenel and Quantico for Atlanta and their mother's family.

As the family is once again in the station wagon, for the first time without their father and without a military base at the end of the trip, Ben wonder if he can "look into the eye of God and spit into that purest source of light for engendering his soul in the seed of a father who did not know the secret of tenderness, a father who loved in strange, undecipherable ways, a father who did not know how to love, a father who did not know how to try?" (469–70). For service men and women, and perhaps especially for Marines, it is almost impossible to storm the beaches in wartime and not bring that same warrior spirit back home, to storm the beaches of his children's lives. Military Brats learn quickly that while they can admire the person who dedicated his or her life to the nation's protection, they can also hate and fear the violent, unpredictable, and distant soldier when he or she comes home. Despite these questions, Ben is "filled up on the road to Atlanta with the love of his father, with the love of Santini" (471). Ben, and Conroy—and most Military Brats—learn to accept this duality between acceptable violence and parental abuse, between rigid discipline and overbearing parenting, between love and hate—both for the person and for the structures that created him.

Sadly, the writing of this book was not initially cathartic for Conroy—or at least not in a positive way. Seltzer notes that after finishing the book, Conroy "spent six months in the grips of an unrelenting depression, making a serious suicide attempt in 1975" (45). This may in part be due to the lingering trauma being exacerbated by reliving it during the process of writing, but it may also be related to the

## Four. "Military brats don't have hometowns"

dilemma Wertsch explores toward the end of her book, when she says that the Brat who tries to tell his or her story to the public is violating a fundamental taboo of military life: that much of it is classified, and nearly all of it should be kept from civilians. Conroy has violated that taboo: he has opened the gate to the Fortress and let the public in; he has shown the devastating results on their families of training men to be warriors.

Unlike Pat Conroy's novel, Bobbie Ann Mason's *In Country* features a female (as opposed to a male) protagonist whose father has been killed in Vietnam before she was born (as opposed to staying alive and torturing her). Also, unlike the other novels discussed in this study, neither Mason nor her protagonist were, strictly speaking, Military Brats. Although Mason spent her childhood in rural Kentucky and had no personal experience with either the Vietnam War or life in the military, she attempts in this novel to show the effects of war on the children of warriors, particularly the warriors who did not survive conflict or were physically and/or psychologically wounded during their service.

As she says in *Patchwork* (a reader), "I did not expect to write a novel about the Vietnam War. During the War, I did not know anyone who went to Vietnam. No personal loss or connection motivated the writing of *In Country*." She adds that although she was "reluctant at first to write about war, I soon realized that war wasn't only battle. It was also the shattering effects on the people at home" (39). According to Joanna Price, her novel won the President's Citation from the Vietnam Veterans of America, "an award given to a non–Vietnam veteran who makes a significant contribution to the veterans' cause" (4). Clearly, Mason's book got something right about the experience of Vietnam veterans and their families to receive such an award, and throughout the years, readers have realized the importance of the story she tells about the ancillary victims of conflict—the children left behind to feel the loss.

When the novel begins, main character Samantha "Sam" Hughes is a high schooler living with her Uncle Emmett, who is also a Vietnam vet. Sam struggles with the ambiguous loss of her father in Vietnam, who died before she was born, and Emmett is dealing, mostly unsuccessfully, with PTSD from his war experiences. To help them both heal, Sam and Emmett decide to take a trip to the Vietnam Memorial. The trip, which is cathartic for Sam and Emmett, frames the main narrative of Sam's struggle to understand and identify with her late father's experiences of the war. Although technically not a Brat, given that her father died before she was born, Sam deals with the combat-induced PTSD experienced by her uncle and other veterans, as do many of the Brats discussed in this book, and, like Conroy's character, she tries to reconcile her father's experiences "in country" with her own adolescent development. Sam's path is to get to know the father she never met by trying to understand and then recreate his experiences at war.

As Joanna Price puts it in her book-length study of the author, the novel is "inscribed with a sense of loss," as Sam tries to "bring to a close the process of mourning for a father whom she has never known." This quest, Price says, "is part of a larger cultural process of mourning that has not, in the mid–1980s, been brought to closure" (57). Thus, Sam became a symbol of the nation's difficulties in coming to terms with the Vietnam War as she engages in her personal quest to know her father. Lisa Hinrichsen says that the novel "interrogates the role memorialization plays in representing the truth of the past and powerfully raises questions of both southern and national memorial practices that prevent the violence that happens elsewhere from ever fully being brought home, showing how even the most average citizens are part of complex systems of historical remembrance, consumption, and erasure" (234–35). That is, Sam shares in these "complex systems" as she tries to both understand and properly memorialize her dead father. Ultimately, the Vietnam Memorial will offer a healing vision that links her life with the lives of the Vietnam veterans, both living and dead.

The first paragraphs of the novel show Sam, Emmett, and Sam's grandmother on the road to Washington, D.C., headed toward the Vietnam Memorial. Sam hopes this trip will help her uncle express some of his repressed emotions about the war when he encounters the memorial, and for Sam, the visit to the memorial is seen as a way of coming to terms with her father's experiences in war and his death.

### Four. "Military brats don't have hometowns"

The narrator summarizes Sam's state of mind, saying that she "feels like letting loose. She has so much evil and bad in her now. It feels good to say *shit*, even if only under her breath" (8). In part, Sam is reckoning with the anger that she never knew her father and with the frustration that no one will talk honestly about him or about the war. It "feels good" for Sam to give voice to these frustrations. On the road, however, Sam also feels "in limbo, stationed right in the center of this enormous amount of energy" (17). She is unsure about how much she wants to know and how the knowledge might change her. As Hinrichsen says, "Mason's novel explores Sam's struggle to access the 'real' past in a post-war world that endlessly reshapes, revises, and reruns it" (235). So, the trip to Washington becomes both real and unreal, cathartic and confusing.

After a brief description of their road trip, the novel returns to Sam's existence before she decided to go on the road. It transpires that Sam is living with her uncle because her mother has moved away to start a new life, and the two of them seem to be stagnating, uncertain how to move forward. The narrator tells readers that Emmett returned alive from Vietnam but "couldn't adjust" (23). He lives in the house that Irene, Sam's mother, bought with the insurance money from her husband's death. Irene treats Emmett "like someone disabled" because the war "messed him up" (23). Emmett responds by staying at home, adopting a caretaking role with Sam and even dressing in skirts, which further alienates him from the people in his smalltown Kentucky home.

Sam, too, seems unable to come to terms with her father and uncle's war. However, watching the final episode of *M\*A\*S\*H* (the wartime comedy set during the Korean War but widely popular in 1972 through 1983, during and after the Vietnam War), she comes to realize that her father was killed in a war (25). Through the mediation of a television series about war (which many saw as an allegory for the Vietnam War), Sam can confront the reality of her father's death. However, she realizes through the course of the novel that she also wants to come to understand his *life*—and his relation to her life. As Harriet Pollack says, "History and herstory are entwined, and Sam—whose name is uncertainly gendered—intertwines her own coming of age with what must have been her father's, structuring a parallel between the unknown dangers he faced in war with those she faces in approaching her own female maturity" (100). Sam's development into a woman is thus coterminous with her understanding of her father's hitherto unknown wartime experiences. Sam, too, finds she is engaged in a "war," a conflict about how she will become a woman and how she will fold her father's experiences into her own development.

However, making this process difficult is the fact that Sam is unable to get her uncle (or anyone else for that matter) to talk honestly about the war, to unburden themselves in the melodramatic way that people do on TV (45). She also realizes that "not every soldier who came back from Vietnam was as weird as Emmett" (46). These men, especially the more quietly traumatized ones, seem reluctant to talk about their war experiences, even if they seemed to have "adjusted perfectly well" (46) to life back home. Sam is also frustrated by the fact that the men she talks to about the war assume that, as a young woman, she cannot fully understand what they've experienced. Sam, whose abbreviated name suggests that she is not particularly comfortable with traditional femininity, is excluded, ironically, by that very femininity from a full accounting of the war. As Jay Watson says, "veterans' rightful access to subject positions where war is concerned also harbors the potential to become a monopoly over them, to reduce those whose bodies are stationed differently relative to war—the men, women, and children who ostensibly 'have not shared the experience' of armed conflict—to the status of uninitiated 'civilians'" (263). Male veterans come to believe that non-combatants, particularly women and children, can never understand what they have experienced. In addition, Watson comments that in the minds of the veterans, "her female body works to disqualify her from any hope of achieving an authentic knowledge of war" (265). By being born female, Sam is prevented from acquiring the knowledge necessary to fully understand what her father (and uncle and other male vets) experienced.

Like the character in Suzanne Collins' children's book, Sam is even confused about what Vietnam *looks* like. From a stamp collection and the tales Emmett told her in childhood, Sam pictures Vietnam as "something like Florida, with beaches and palm trees and

## Four. "Military brats don't have hometowns"

watery fields of rice and green mountains" (51). Her mother stopped the stories because she believed they upset her daughter, but, in actuality, they gave Sam some sort of picture—albeit romanticized—of where her father fought and died. When Sam finally saw footage of the Fall of Saigon (1975) on TV, "for the first time, Vietnam was an actual place" (51). Sam admonishes her for not telling her more about Vietnam and her father's experience there (56). Her mother replies that Sam "fret[s] too much" about Vietnam and incorrectly assumes that it "had nothing to do with" her daughter (57). As she moves into adulthood, Sam starts to feel that Vietnam *does* have something to do with her, although she is not quite sure what. As Price says, Sam "searches for a 'map' that will enable her to read what happened to her father in Vietnam, and by knowing this, to accommodate the otherness that the Vietnamese landscape and people represent to her" (62). The novel becomes her search for that "map."

Looking at the only picture of her father she has, which was taken when he was the age of Sam's boyfriend Lonnie, Sam "couldn't see any resemblance to him" (58). Sam wants to connect visually and emotionally with her father, but she is finding it difficult. "The soldier boy in the picture never changed," the narrator says. "In a way that made him dependable. But he seemed so innocent" (66). She stares at the picture but concludes that her father "had died with his secrets" (67). Her father's picture will not speak to her, it will not change, and it, along with the Vietnam vets she knows, will not offer her any useful explanation of the war.

Sam tells Lonnie that although her mother tells her the war didn't have anything to do with her, she feels it "had *everything* to do with me. My daddy went over there to fight for Mom's sake, and Emmett went over there for Mom's sake and my sake, to get revenge.... The ones who don't get killed come back with their lives messed up, and then they make everybody miserable" (71). Sam realizes, from personal experience, that when a man goes off to war, claiming to be doing it to protect his family, he runs the risk of destroying that family in the process. War, in Sam's mind, has everything to do with the wives and children left at home, since they are the excuses men give for going to fight.

## Brat Life

In her frustrated attempts to understand her father's war experience, Sam seeks a relationship with an older veteran, Tom, who tells her that she "might as well just stop asking questions about the war. Nobody gives a shit. They've got it twisted around in their heads what it was about, so they can live with it and not have to think about it" (79). People who stayed home, Tom says, come up with narratives that serve their own purposes, but which also deny the reality of veteran's experiences. "Nobody understands the vets," Sam tells Lonnie. "They're different. People expect them to behave like everybody else, but they can't" (87). Although she does not understand the profundity of the effects of the Vietnam War on those who fought in it, Sam realizes that the war changed her uncle and the other vets, just as it might have changed her father if he had survived.

Certainly, Sam's life is different than it would have been if her father had not been killed in Vietnam. The narrator says that Sam "was feeling the delayed stress of the Vietnam War. It was her inheritance" (89). However, she cannot find a way to cope with that "inheritance" or how to help other vets in her life. Nothing, including the paltry records at the courthouse, can tell her anything about what the war experience was like for her father, and, by extension, who she is. Sam finds it "maddening" that "no one knew anything but the obvious" (118–119). Shortly after her trip to the courthouse, Sam thinks about "all the lives wasted by the war.... All the boys getting killed, on both sides. And boys getting mutilated. And then not being allowed to grow up" (140). To understand the war, Sam has been, as Michael Barry puts it, ineffectively "probing communal memory in an attempt to satisfy herself and heal herself" (142). None of these methods work, though, and Sam grows increasingly desperate to find out something meaningful about her father—and about war.

At this point of maximum confusion, Sam finds her father's wartime letters to her mother. She discovers that her father wanted a boy, and she realizes that her father might have been withholding crucial information from his young wife. "Her father must have been very brave," Sam thinks, but he was "just trying to protect Irene—and by extension, years later, her. The dead took their secrets with them. She wondered how far to go in honoring the dead if the dead offer you

## Four. "Military brats don't have hometowns"

nothing except a little mindless protection, by keeping their secrets from you" (182). This "mindless protection" is maddening to Sam, as it impedes her quest to understand her father, herself, and the complex legacies of war. As an adolescent and no longer a child, Sam does not want to be protected from the truth.

As a result of her looking into her father's war experiences through reading his letters and studying books on Vietnam, Sam starts to identify with him, feeling that "the jungle was closing in, and even the maple trees on Maple Street seemed as though they might be hiding snipers" (184). She also realizes that also she wants "to care about her father, but she didn't know enough about him" (191). As she learns how little she knows about her father, Sam discovers that he knew nothing about her, either. Sam looks around her father's family farm, and she thinks that his childhood "was small and predictable" (200). The world, which now has Sam in it, the world of rock videos and *M*A*S*H*, has passed her teenaged father by. He never had a chance to grow into the adulthood toward which Sam is headed.

At this point, her father's mother gives Sam her father's diary, which is much franker about her father's war experiences than his letters home. Sam is disgusted by the vivid descriptions of death and the realities of war in his diary: "Now everything seemed suddenly so real it enveloped her, like something rotten she had fallen into" (206). The rottenness of the Vietnam experience has finally penetrated Sam's consciousness, and she feels tainted by it. Things may be getting too real, by far.

After being disturbed by the diary, Sam decides to simulate wartime conditions at Cawood's Pond, a local park near her home. Sam thinks, "If men went to war for women, and for unborn generations, then she was going to find out what they went through" (208). During this stay, she concludes that "men were nostalgic about killing. It aroused something in them" (209). Women, she thinks, "didn't kill. That was why her mother wouldn't honor the flag or honor the dead. She concludes that "whenever she had tried to imagine Vietnam she had had her facts all wrong" (210). She concludes: "She thought of tanks knocking down the jungle and tigers sitting under bushes. Her notions came from the movies. Some vets blamed what they did on the horror of the jungle. What did the jungle do to them? Humping the boonies. Here I am, she thought. In country" (210).

Ultimately, Sam realizes that her trip to the woods was not equivalent to her father's time in country. Emmett comes to find her and reinforces what she fears is true: "I know why you were out here," he says. "You think you can go through what we went through out in the jungle, but you can't." He continues, "It's childish, to go run off to the wilderness to get revenge. It's the most typical thing in the world" (221). In Emmett's mind, Sam's trip to the swamp is a childish stunt enacted by a girl who has never faced any real danger in her life. However, as Hinrichsen says, Sam "wants to know not what happened, but what it was like; for this understanding, affect is a crucial dimension of experience" (243). Sam needs this visceral experience, contrived as it is, to feel what her father felt in country. As Watson puts it, Sam's "epiphanies cumulatively indicate that a young woman may come to know plenty about war simply by inhabiting her own gendered and eminently vulnerable, pregnable body" (284). As a young woman, Sam, too, is in danger—from sexual assault, from unwanted pregnancy, from the micro aggressions that women experience every day. It may not be an actual war, but it often feels like conflict and can result in lasting trauma.

Sam retorts that her father and Emmett's enlistments were equally childish. She tells her uncle, "That explains what the whole country was doing over there. The least little threat and America's got to put on its cowboy boots and stomp around and show somebody a thing or two" (221). Under the guise of patriotism, men went off to war to "stomp around and show somebody a thing or two." Emmett angrily responds, "You can't do what we did and then be happy about it. And nobody lets you forget it. Goddamn it, Sam!" (222). Emmett may have gone to war to avenge his friend's life, but he returned damaged internally and stigmatized externally. He adds, "You can't learn from the past. The main thing you learn from history is that you can't learn from history. That's what history is" (226). In Emmett's mind, Sam cannot learn anything useful from studying (and trying to vicariously experience) the war.

### Four. "Military brats don't have hometowns"

Still, the trip changes Sam. After coming back from the pond, Sam feels like she doesn't fit in: "None of it pertained to her.... The soldiers must have felt like that, as though they belonged nowhere" (231). Through her time "humping the boonies," she has internalized some of the alienation experienced by veterans. While visiting a mall on their trip, "Sam stands transfixed by the trees and the thick foliage. They become the jungle plants of Southeast Asia. And then they change to cypress trees at Cawood's Pond, and the murky swamp water, infested with snakes, swirls around her" (237). Emmett may not recognize it, but Sam has found a way to travel to Vietnam, to absorb the experiences of being in country.

When they finally get to the Vietnam Memorial at the end of the novel, they find her father's name, and Sam also discovers someone with her name on the wall: "How odd it feels, as though all the names in America have been used to decorate this wall" (245). As Susan Jeffords says, "She represents all of those who have been excluded and are now brought back. That Sam and America can only join in this masculine bond through a name carved in stone suggests the rigidly of positions defined by the bond. Now dead and reborn as 'Sam Alan Hughes,' Samantha Hughes is no longer excluded from Vietnam" (64). By having her name masculinized and place on the Wall, Sam is now able to be a part of the experience that had hitherto been denied her.

Emmett, too, seems partially healed by the experience, and in the final sentence of the novel, readers see him "sitting there cross legged in front of the wall" as his face "bursts into a smile like flames" (245). Because of this trip, Sam, too, can see the ways in which she fits into the Vietnam experience. Her name, her father's name, the name of one of Emmett's buddies all adorn the Wall. By losing a father and then coming to know him more fully, Sam has realized that the war came home with the veterans in her hometown, with her uncle, with the remains of her father, and it came home in her. As Allison M. Johnson says, Sam "must masculinize herself to fit into the war's and the wall's rhetoric" (1). As she sees her own name on the Wall, Sam becomes a veteran. Eventually, Johnson comments, the trauma of the war "writes itself onto Sam and she carries the burden of Vietnam by not only being surrounded by these men, but also by assuming the trauma of their experiences as her own" (2). In touching "her" name on the Wall, Johnson says, "Sam wins her place among veterans primarily by getting in touch with herself, her own body" (286). Touch is key: she must experience "humping the boonies" at Cawood's Pond, and she must feel her own name on the Wall. After all, Johnson points out, "Sam exists because of war, her own moment of origin a complex interweaving of sexual and military exigencies" (290). Sam is both a product and a victim of the Vietnam War.

This may be a bit more complicated, though. Price says, "despite her sense of recognition, Samantha Hughes' name is not identical to the name of the wall, which suggests that the historical construction of sexual difference cannot be so easily overcome" (82). Finding a version of her name may not be enough to overcome gender differences regarding war experiences. However, Hinrichsen says that the novel "concludes with a kind of volatile meeting between private memory and public memory as the wall of the memorial functions to present the problem of representing recent traumas: namely, the continued involvement of the observing subject, the ways in which we are still part of the processes and practices that generated the Vietnam conflict" (246). This "volatile meeting" of the observed (the names of the dead) and the observer (in this case Sam and her family) is the only pathway to understanding. Johnson says, "Sam Hughes' story of war and the body, war *on* the body, is ultimately a clarion call to all Americans for find and articulate their own" (304). As Sam comes to terms with her personal Vietnam story, the rest of us must find a way to incorporate war into our personal and collective consciousness.

Sam Hughes may not be a typical Military Brat, but she is the child of a warrior, and she bears the legacy of loss, of uncertainty, of fear that many Brats experience. She may not have known her father, but she has a need to understand him, to know why he went to fight and what he experienced while in country. Sam struggles with a ghost of her father, rather than the violent or absent living fathers most Brats contend with, but she encounters the alienating effects of the Fortress on her own attempts to understand the military and what it does to its members.

Unlike *In Country*, the protagonist of Elizabeth Berg's novels

*Four.* "*Military brats don't have hometowns*"

(*Durable Goods* and its companion novels *Joy School* and *True to Form*) has a living father who is still in the military. Like *In Country* and in contrast to *The Great Santini*, Elizabeth Berg's works look at this insular world of the Fortress from the focal point of a daughter instead of a son. Although some of the issues change if the child is female, as Wertsch shows, the stresses of moving, of having an unpredictable parent, and of never having one's needs acknowledged are the same. In an interview with the author printed at the back of *True to Form*, Berg says that "Katie is the character most like me—over-sensitive, dreamy, enamored of the written word, full of longing" (NP). Like Conroy, Berg seems compelled to tell this story—which is also her story—and to reap the rewards and assume the risks associated with the telling.

*Durable Goods*, the first novel in the series, opens with the main character, 12-year-old Katie (who has recently lost her mother to cancer), preparing for yet another move. Her father "doesn't like to hear complaining about the way we move so much," and Katie and her sister "are not allowed to cry when we drive away—or at any other time, either—about any place we leave behind" (48). After arriving at a new place, Katie "can call back the sadness to let it out. But sometimes it has gone somewhere. You have not lost it, just the ability to get rid of it by crying. It will be a part of you now, steal up on you at unexpected moments" (49). This sorrow, this loss, becomes "a part of you," and by not being expressed at the time, it becomes something that cannot be assuaged by tears. Katie's conclusion is that she does not believe the Army "is a good idea for people with regular human hearts" (63). What she means is that children who are uprooted frequently, and who are admonished not to express sadness at those displacements, learn not to feel the loss; they learn to detach from homes, from friends, and from emotions. This detachment comes at a price, however, and that is in strained connections with their families.

On learning that they are moving again, Katie feels surprised, which makes sense, given that she has learned not to dwell on the sadness of leaving and the inevitability of life in a new place. "Each time, you learn a place forgetting that you must leave it. Each time, there is a pulling-away pain when it is time to go" (113). The Brat cannot dwell on the inevitable ending if she or he is trying to adapt, to fit in. She also knows that she will feel the familiar fear of entering, once again, a new classroom. She concludes, "It is too hard to do this so often. Really, it is too hard" (114). Even though it is "too hard," Katie knows that she will have to do it—once again. Perhaps being surprised every time is a kind of coping mechanism, a way of trying to keep the pain from accumulating.

Thinking back, Katie remembers her father telling her mother to buy "durable goods; that's what's going to make it" (132). Applied literally, this means the sturdier and plainer the furniture, the less likely it is to be damaged or stolen in the frequent moves. Applied metaphorically, this means that family members should become "durable" as well: serviceable but plain, battered but strong, to hold up to frequent disruptions. However, Katie says that having more delicate things, which her mother loves, are worth the risk. Even if some things get broken, many of these breakable objects remain intact, and each time they unpack, and grieve over what is broken, the members of the family "are glad to see a frying pan with a curved handle your hand already knows. You are glad to have your own same bed back again, your old clothes hung in the new closet. You flip through the pages of your books before you put them away. In the lonely first few weeks, you take all you can from your old things" (132–33). It is difficult to convey to those in the civilian world what household goods—durable or not—come to mean in the lives of Army Brats. They are the only continuity between the life before and the life after; they *are* the family in a family that lacks a hometown and a familiar family home. If they are dented or even if some of them are broken, they are—even battered and scuffed—all that you have to remind you who you are.

This is the best-case scenario; another more distressing outcome is that all your possessions could be lost in the move or confiscated by the country from which you and your family had to flee, as when military families had to leave everything behind in Iran at the start of the Islamic Revolution (when the U.S.-backed Shah of Iran was deposed). For those families and the countless others that had to leave a war-torn country at a moment's notice, there will be no familiar frying pans or beloved books waiting at the new posting.

Brats may attempt to hold on to household goods, to memories,

### Four. "Military brats don't have hometowns"

and to places, but eventually they fade, and "you start making it up. You know you're getting things wrong, but you make it up to not lose it all. And it's like the places want to try, too. They jump into your head, a scene every now and then, like the too-bright light of a camera: your hallway, here, *flash*: don't forget. The line of bushes in your front yard, here, *flash*: don't forget. All of it fails. All of it fades" (142). All that many Brats can hold onto are these flashes of places they left long ago. Still, there is a desire to hold onto the past, to leave a mark. On the last day in their house in Texas, Katie notes the "marks on the walls, evidence of how we were. It is the loneliest thing, to see those last pieces of you that stay behind" (186). This house will soon be filled by other Brats, who will likely notice the traces Katie and her father left behind, as they are adjusting to *their* next new place.

In the car on their way to a new assignment, the family stops at an A&W root beer stand. Katie hears "the inviting rattle of glasses, smell[s] the hamburgers. And now there is my father's voice, his hand lightly touching my arm. 'Hey, wake up,' he is saying. 'Everything is here'" (192). Of course, her father does not actually say this directly—he is a military man, after all—but Katie senses that he is telling her that family is all that matters, that they have "everything" when they are together. This is a lovely sentiment, but a family that is everything to you can come to feel like a prison, especially if that family is violent, unpredictable, or otherwise damaged.

In the Reader's Guide to *Durable Goods*, Berg says that she "meant only to write about being an army brat. What emerged was a story about compassion—the need for it, the expression of it. I also learned a lot about what my feelings for my father are. I grew up afraid of him, but I came to understand that his heart is huge and that he is in fact a very sensitive man. I would have to say that I return to compassion in many if not all of my books. And the importance of friendship. Most of all, I want to show the great glory in our ordinary lives, in our ordinary selves" (199). Like Pat Conroy, Berg (like Katie) was afraid of her father, but she did come to recognize his huge heart under all the military bluster. In her novels, Berg captures the "great glory" of ordinary life in the military, but she also shows the loss and the loneliness of Brat life.

## Brat Life

*Joy School* picks up where *Durable Goods* leaves off. Katie and her father have moved to Missouri, where she forms a friendship with the unpopular Cynthia and the popular but reckless Taylor. She also develops an unrequited crush on a 23-year-old gas station attendant. Many of the same concerns reflected in *Durable Goods* reappear in this novel. In this work, Katie struggles to adapt to a new place, confronts the complicated nature of memory, and deals with her emotionally distant and sometimes volatile father.

Early in the story, Katie fruitlessly complains to her father about not liking their new place, and then she notices her dog, Bridgette, who is happy with her bone: "There are ways of not needing much," she thinks (24). This is the struggle of many Military Brats: their complaints about frequent postings and subsequent dislocations and uncertainty are met with incomprehension or are dismissed as irrelevant. The only choice, then, is to find ways of "not needing much." This is the classic hallmark of insecure attachment: the child who has learned not to depend on the stability of her family finds ways not to notice what she has never had. She also contrasts her life to that of her friend, Cynthia, who has her identity firmly fixed in her familiar house and unchanging family situation. Cynthia has an identity connected in part to place, but all that Cynthia knows about Katie is that she is an "army brat from Texas" (31). This is all many civilian children know about Military Brats, who move in and out of their towns on a regular basis.

Katie's father's anger is only marginally more under control in this novel. When her father reprimands her for going to Cynthia's house without asking him, although she has gotten permission from their housekeeper, Ginger, Katie thinks, "I am not ready to take on the load of this. He has been so much better lately, I'd forgotten how he can turn. The thing to do is get past him, let it soak in that I am home now, he can be done" (42). The hypervigilance of the military life contributes, in part, to her father's reluctance to let her out of his immediate control, even though he is rarely around to keep an eye on her himself. Both Katie and her father have a heightened sense of the dangers of the world; he worries about violence done by others to his daughter, and she worries about the violence done by him. Behind this is the inherent violence of the military world they inhabit.

### Four. "Military brats don't have hometowns"

When her pregnant older sister, who has left home to be with her boyfriend, returns for Thanksgiving with him (who is now her husband), her father is furious. Katie thinks that she "feel[s] sorry for him. I wish I could tell him to go in my room, but that would be taking sides and my father would just get madder. When he is like this, he welcomes more to keep him going" (74). Like the children in *The Great Santini* and those in many of the nonfictional stories of Brat life, Military Brats must anticipate their father's anger, avoid it if possible, and manage it if not. This parentification of Brats is something mentioned by Wertsch and the psychologists quoted in other chapters of this study. When Katie's sort-of friend Taylor, who is a "slinky chameleon," comes to dinner, Taylor manages to tease and cajole Katie's father into something resembling relaxation. "To tell the truth," Katie thinks, "I really enjoyed it. It was relaxing. I thought, when did I ever before feel this way at my dinner table? The answer was, never" (171). Katie has never enjoyed a dinner with her father because she never knows when he will erupt in anger or issue commands that she will have to obey. Unless she is willing to be infinitely adaptable, like Taylor, to conceal her true self, she will never be completely safe from his anger.

Still, there is a positive aspect to having such a controlling and dominating father. For example, only her father can get Ginger's large dog under control: "That is the thing about strong people," Katie thinks. "You can mostly be scared of them but sometimes the way they are makes you feel safe" (108). Katie, like many other Brats, seems willing, at least sometimes, to trade peace for safety. And given the dangers that are so readily apparent to children living with warriors, Katie quickly realizes that she needs safety over relaxation. She may fear her father, but if he is strong enough, she may not have to fear other perils—like nuclear annihilation or the overthrow of democracy.

This does not mean that Katie believes that life in the military is a good one, however. When she thinks about her father's job as an Army recruiter, Katie cannot imagine how he convinces young men to join: "What can he say? Here's where you'll live!!! Here's what you'll wear!!! I understand they can get their school paid for, maybe that's a reason they sign up. As for me, I'd work somewhere, save up and pay for it myself so it was mine clean. I could tell those young men about the drill sergeants I have heard so clearly outside my window where we used to live" (127).

From hard experience, Katie knows that life in the military is not just housing, reduced-price groceries, uniforms, and paid college tuition. It involves being willing to sacrifice your life after being willing to submit yourself to the humiliations and transformations of boot camp. Of course, as Wertsch has shown, certain kinds of men choose the military for those transformations; they want to submit themselves to an authority and a purpose above themselves. However, Brats do not have that option; they are told where they will live, how they will act, and how to keep silent about the violence and dysfunction at home.

The third novel in this series, *True to Form*, takes place in the summer of 1961. Now 13-year-old Katie has been forced by her father to take two summer jobs: as babysitter and as a companion to a bedridden woman. She is also coerced into joining a Girl Scout troop by the mother of her best friend Cynthia. She keeps in touch by letter with her friend Cherylanne from a previous posting, and when she wins a radio contest, she takes a short but unsatisfying trip back to see her. Cherylanne, who is older than Katie, has gotten pregnant and plans to marry her boyfriend. This book focuses much of its attention to Katie's trip back to see her friend in Texas and on the uncertainties of military life.

Early in the novel, Katie thinks about her relatively new room: "I am used to it now, which probably means it's about time to move. Every time I get used to something, it's time to leave it. 'We have orders,' my father will say, and that's that, we're on the way to wherever the army tells us to go" (4). It should be noted that these are called "orders"; they are not suggestions or options, and, as Katie has discovered, it does no good to complain about them. "Here's how much my opinion counts: Zero. My opinion is called talking back" (12). There is no point in arguing about what the military has ordered, and there is very little point in feeling sad about it.

This does not mean that the Military Brat is ever psychologically comfortable with the frequent dislocations. One result of this is that places where one has lived in the past take on a certain unreality. As

## Four. "Military brats don't have hometowns"

Katie puts it, "I would really like, for once in my life, to go back to a place I used to live, which I have never been able to do. Sometimes it seems like I just made those places up" (20). This is part of the mental gymnastics in which Brats engage: the past becomes unreal, unreachable, unmissable. She elaborates on this dilemma: "When your dad is in the army, it's like you're always saying, 'Okay, this is home.' And then, 'No. *This* is home.' And so on and so on forever. But the joke is that you are never home except inside yourself. That is where you have to make the place where the light is always on, a chair *always* waiting, *sit down*. It is always the same light, and it is always the same chair, turned just so and never moving one inch" (53). As a necessity, Brats learn to create a home inside themselves, where the light is always on, and the familiar chair is always where you left it. Either that, or they tell themselves that they do not need a stable and familiar home, that they are just fine with the "adventure" of moving.

Going back to where she used to live in Texas, even briefly, makes Katie "feel strong" (65). However, when she gets there, she realizes that she does not belong there anymore. "It's not a sad feeling, or a bad one. It's like a page turned in a notebook you will always keep, but now you are on the new page. I think something in me knew that I had to see this place again to understand that" (74). Although she says that this does not make her feel sad or bad, it does color her view of the world. She says that she knows "one thing," and that is that "anything we have, we are only borrowing. Anything. Any time" (72). This is a worldview shared by many Military Brats: everything in your life, including having a father, can change or even disappear at any minute. Even when she does get to visit a former home, she does not find herself there.

Like Berg's novels and the others in this chapter, Sarah Bird's *The Yokota Officers Club* is set in the period between the 1950s and the 1970s. Main character Bernadette "Bernie" Root is one of six siblings, who include brothers Buzz, Abner, Bob, Bosco, and sister Kit. Their father is an Air Force pilot and a major, and their mother, Moe, is a housewife. At the beginning of the novel, Bernie has arrived at Kadena Air Base in Okinawa, Japan, where her family is now stationed, after a year at college. Like Conroy, and his fictional alter ego, Ben, Bernie is the child of a pilot who demands obedience and has a hair-trigger temper. Also like Ben and the other characters—both real and fictional—discussed in this study, Bernie struggles with the demands placed on her as a Military Brat.

For example, as she travels to Kadena, Bernie thinks about moving much like most Military Brats. She especially likes "the part after the packers left but before I became the new girl," calling it "the coziest time in my life. Just me and the sibs and Moe, sealed up in our mobile incubator hurtling down the highway." The best part about this is that there are "no Outsiders. Outsiders—which is to say, anyone that Moe had not brought into this world—and my family did not mix" (6). As should be obvious by now, this is a common attitude of Military Brats: the family is the most important thing in their lives, their only constant, and anyone else is an "outsider." While this can be "cozy," it can also be a breeding ground for family secrets of all kinds, and, as in the Conroy household, this "mobile incubator" can breed violence and abuse.

Bernie also thinks about a memo to service men and women written by then-president (and former military general) Dwight D. Eisenhower: "Service men and women are the largest group of official U.S. personnel stationed in foreign countries. As a result, people form their personal attitudes toward our country and our American way of life to a great extent by what they see and hear about American service personnel and their dependents" (11). The "and dependents" is key: not only do the service members have to assume that they represent the United States, but also so do their dependents, which in the military includes the spouses as well. The wives and children are both dependent *and* representative, unable to control their futures and under pressure to be good examples to the world.

On arriving at the airport at Kadena, Bernie looks out on a landscape that will be familiar to most Military Brats—the base: "Cinder-block walls are painted a dispirited tan. Standing ashtrays are made of hundred-pound bombs. Arrows stenciled in black on the walls order me unequivocally toward the reception area. Other signs bark out acronyms, squadron names, unit designations, the whole vast hieroglyphic that orchestrates every twitch of military life" (19).

## Four. "Military brats don't have hometowns"

Ashtrays made of bomb casings, orders in the form of navigational signs, and cinderblock buildings are all part of the "vast hieroglyphic that orchestrates every twitch of military life." This is a utilitarian life with the sole purpose of preparing for war. Perhaps even more importantly for a female Brat, this is a world surrounded by "overwhelming hordes" of young men. This theatrical and carefully-scripted world is not one that knows what to do with women and girls, or, at least, not with the mothers and daughters of service men. The women in the community serve as maids and as sex workers to those "hordes."

Upon arriving at her family's quarters, Bernie finds that her siblings have changed in the year she's been away from them, but her father looks "precisely" the same: "He stands ramrod straight in starched khakis, his hair in a crew cut, black shoes shined to a mirror finish, the smell of Brasso wafting off his polished belt buckle. It doesn't appear that his weight has fluctuated more than six ounces or his hair been allowed to grow an extra millimeter" (23). This is the model of the military officer: polished, starched, straight, and perfectly controlled. The military father appearance may be the only constant in a Brat's life, but he is often the source of fear and unpredictability as well. He will continue to look the same on the outside, and he will continue to be as unstable as ever on the inside.

As she settles in, Bernie soon hears what she calls the "hyperkinetic Armed Forces Radio voice [that] comes from the very near yet irretrievably lost past. It is a past that lives on, here in Okinawa, the keystone of the Pacific" (40). This base, like many others, seems lost in the past. Despite the protests against the Vietnam War going on back at home (and outside the bases overseas as well), Okinawa seems "like a *Twilight Zone* episode with all the massed forces of the military combined to maintain the illusion that the America I just left has not changed forever. That the country everyone on this tiny island has been sent to defend is still back there, everyone listening to the same happy tunes" (40). This is the paramount illusion of military bases, especially those in foreign countries. This world is orderly, locked in the past, and dedicated to serving the needs of military members and their dependents—and to keeping out the messy and changing world.

## Brat Life

Later in the novel, when she attends "Kadina Karnival," Bernie finds herself "circling a parade ground in a hay wagon pulled by a tank while I slurp a Coke and snitch French fries as a Marine band plays Sousa marches in the distance. It is Americana in a concentration known to few who have not experienced the overseas military base" (122). It is an odd sort of "Americana," though, one in which the wagons are pulled by tanks and a Marine band plays in the background.

The interior world of a military officer is very different, though, from the external show of unchanging American patriotism. Bernie realizes that her "father lives in a more vivid world than most, where each day is a series of agonistic encounters against a host of enemies ... all bent on his destruction" (47). This is a world that precludes complaints, disobedience, even minor disruptions, not just on the part of the service person but also on the part of dependents as well. Her father achieves this focus in part by going to work and to bed early. It appears to Bernie that "he simply prefers living in a different time zone from us, from his family" (57). If the service member can avoid, as much as possible, the messiness and distractions of family life, he or she can more easily engage in his or her "series of agonistic encounters against a host of enemies." Like Pat Conroy's father, Bernie's dad lives "in a different time zone" from his family, one that will allow him to disengage from them at any moment, which he may well be required to do. It is also a world where the primary mission is kept hidden.

All the men living on base leave their dependents behind, segregated in the area devoted to base housing. This is a world in which denial is paramount, a world in which its most obvious feature is "the complete lack, during working hours, of any male over the age of eighteen," no grandparents except on rare visits, no mailmen, and no outside dogs (75). As Bernie puts it, "We're floating on this beautiful balloon of an island where no one mentions nuclear weapons or Vietnam. Where troublesome teens and their families simply vanish overnight" (81). They are on a literal and metaphorical island, Okinawa, where to acknowledge the brutal realities of occupation and war would make life impossible. However, at the end of this "idyllic" picture is the harsh reality: anyone who is "troublesome" will disappear along

## Four. "Military brats don't have hometowns"

with her family. This is not an exaggeration: children who chronically get into trouble often damage their serving parent's career, and the most serious cases cause the entire family to be expelled from this "paradise."

Soon after Bernie arrives, her father confronts her about her college participation in protests against the Vietnam War, which, presumably, he has been informed about by military intelligence. Needless to say, he is not pleased: "Before a young woman who has been housed, clothed, and fed her entire life by the United States government criticizes that government, wouldn't you imagine she should have an exceptionally clear, and exceptionally *precise* idea of what it is she's protesting?" (104), he asks. The assumption here is that she owes the military her loyalty and that once she has fully understood the reasons why the military is in Vietnam, she will cease protesting the war (and bringing shame on her father).

When her father leaves on TDY (temporary duty), a common occurrence during wartime, Bernie's mother takes over the running of the household. Bernie thinks, "Seeing that old animation is startling. It is as if she's been lying in wait for our father to leave so she could take over again" (108). Like fictional Ben and real-life Conroy's mother, Moe is invigorated by having her husband away. Finally, the military wife has a purpose, which is to hold down the fort until the service member returns. Shortly after this, Bernie gets a job as a backup dancer with a musical/comedy show that tours officers' clubs throughout Asia, and the tour itinerary includes Yokota Air Force Base, where she lived "on the economy" as a child in the 1950s near the base with their local maid, Fumiko.

Reflecting upon her family's earlier arrival in Japan, Bernie remembers that the family "drove onto Yokota Air Base and my lungs expanded with the first full breath I'd taken since we left Travis [Air Force Base]. Everything that was wrong about Japan was right here. The streets were broad and calm. Trees stood in tall, straight columns; cars were blue, red, green, yellow. An American flag snapped overhead. A barbed-wire fence with a guard at the gate embraced it all. This was home. This was where I wanted to stay" (186–7). This is typical of the Brat experience: no matter how chaotic a country one has landed in, the base will always be an island of security and order. Seeing Yokota again, Bernie longs for the peace and security of her past as a young Brat.

However, when music promoter Bobby asks if she is nervous about playing her "hometown" of Yakota AFB, she angrily responds that Yakota is not her hometown: "A hometown is where you go back and they remember you from when you were a kid. This is like being Jewish and going back to Krakow or something. All the buildings are the same, but everyone you every knew is dead or PCS'd [Permanent Change of Station], which amounts to the same thing. For me, Yakota is a fully populated ghost town" (266). This may be the best description available of the Military Brats' relationship with the bases that they are relieved to enter and inevitably leave. The human beings come and go, and the bases remain as "ghost towns" for those who have left. No friends or family remain to visit; only the memories are constant. The mention of Krakow is interesting: Bernie clearly feels as if she was in a kind of ghetto, one she was forced to enter and to which she never developed an attachment. No one she knows is there anymore, and all traces of her stay have been eradicated. There are no hometowns for these transient people, either those in enforced ghettoes or Brats on military bases.

Towards the end of the novel, Bernie reflects on what happens after the fathers go on a mission: toddlers start regressing on toilet training, and older children start showing up at the dispensary with an array of psychosomatic disorders (318–19). As various studies of military children and their mothers have uncovered, psychological and psychosomatic complaints arise when the military member is deployed. The struggles are not confined to smaller children, however: older children begin to break the rules and engage in petty vandalism (319).

Again, as studies have revealed, sexual escapades and incidences of petty crimes like vandalism and shoplifting rise when the fathers are absent. Even those young adults who continue to abide by most rules will break the habit of following protocol, refusing to stand during the National Anthem at the theater, for example. Their mothers are not well, either, buying "ninety-six-piece sets of Noritake

## Four. "Military brats don't have hometowns"

china and smoky topaz cocktail rings, geisha dolls in tall glass cases, and beaten brass coffee tables they didn't need and couldn't afford. And they drank" (319). Heavy-drinking mothers with shopping addictions are not particularly stable caretakers, as demonstrated by the other fictional and nonfictional accounts of Brat life examined in this study. Each of the family members left behind struggles to gain control, or to numb their feelings, in any way possible. When Bernie's mother complains that she did not enlist in military life, another officer's wife tells her, "Don't kid yourself. You signed up the day you let him put a ring on your finger. We all did" (322). Wives, unlike the children of warriors, might have had some choice in whether to marry the military (as spouses are encouraged to think about it), but unless they were Brats themselves, they have no idea what they are getting themselves into.

At the novel ends, Bernie thinks about the pilots who are also fathers and the secret they share: "Only they knew that their families and all the families of American were safe that night because they had put their lives on the line and won.... The golden light they were bathed in that made them look like heroes came from the simple fact that they were heroes" (340). Like Pat Conroy and his fictional alter ego Ben and the rest of the Brats discussed in this study, it is often impossible for children to challenge these "heroes." Nor can they fail to love and admire them, regardless of their shortcomings as fathers and husbands. These men are "golden." They are "heroes," which may make up for their not being very good parents.

Bernie's father the Air Force pilot, Katie's father the Army soldier, and Ben's father the Marine pilot are all seen as heroes by their children, and they often see themselves in this light. Or if they do not, they envision themselves engaged in a life-and-death struggle to defend the nation. These fathers have sacrificed their individuality for duty and their lives for their country. They also struggle to balance heroism with the mundane and often annoying aspects of marriage and family. They have little patience for complaints and *no* patience for disorder or disloyalty. They take their children from house to house, from state to state, from country to country. They separate them from their friends and from their extended families, and they demand nothing less than absolute obedience. After all, what their children sacrifice pales in comparison to what they have sworn to give up for their country.

So, what is the purpose of these sometimes angry and often despondent novels? Will they inspire Brat readers with their compassion and their insights? Will they reach others outside the military community who can identify because of their own trauma and abuse? Will they lead to meaningful change within and without the military? Highly doubtful, given the nature of the military and its need to prioritize the mission over the man and certainly over the family. Still, an exploration of the "ordinary traumas" of life for Military Brats can encourage Brats to treat themselves with more compassion and may, perhaps, spur family organizations within the military to consider what might be done to make their lives more peaceful and more secure. Bernie, Katie, Sam, and Ben's stories offer current and former Brats the comforting message that they are not alone, that the sorrow and fear they felt throughout their childhoods have been and are still being shared by others. Perhaps it will also encourage those within the Fortress to pay more attention to the needs of military children, even when those children are insisting that they are just fine. Maybe the military can work harder at creating a home for these homeless children.

# Five

# "A Secure Base"
## *Famous Brats and Their Life Stories*

> Make a grave for the unknown soldier
> Nestled in your hollow shoulder
> The unknown soldier
> —"Unknown Soldier," The Doors

When one Googles "famous military brats," one finds that the list is long and that it includes actors, musicians, politicians, writers, and even gurus. Some have lived chaotic lives; others have been quietly successful; and still others have influenced the world stage politically in ways that might be perceived as both good and bad. Of course, there is no single life pattern for Military Brats who have become famous, but some familiar threads emerge if one studies the lives of these well-known military children. For the purposes of this chapter, I have chosen to focus on Brats who have entered creative fields like music and writing, as well as a politician and the founder of a controversial religion, just for good measure. Through examining the stories of L. Ron Hubbard (Navy), Jim Morrison (Navy). Newt Gingrich (Army), and Suzanne Collins (Air Force), it becomes possible to see how their experiences of rootlessness, authoritarian and/or absent fathers, and uncertainty about the future have affected these famous Brats in ways very similar to those previously discussed in fiction and the autobiographies of the less well-known ones.

To make the claim that childhood experiences like parental military service affect the development of children and thereby their behaviors and emotions as adults, it is necessary to look at theories of human development such as those elaborated by pioneering psychologists in child development like Uri Bronfenbrenner and John Bowlby. As Bronfenbrenner says in *The Ecology of Human Development* (1979), "Understanding of *human* [as opposed to animal] development demands more than direct observation of behavior on the part of one or two persons in the same place; it requires examination of multiperson systems of interaction not limited to a single setting and must take into account aspects of the environment beyond the immediate situation containing the subject" (21). That is, direct observation of an individual, or of a single relationship in a person's life, is not enough to fully understand their motivations and the resulting behaviors in both childhood and adulthood. The key here is that this multi-person system, operating in a variety of settings, is a "growing, dynamic entity that progressively moves into and restructures the milieu in which it resides" (21). Development is changing both the individual and the larger social systems in which that person lives. According to Lawrence Shelton, who in 2019 authored a primer summarizing Bronfenbrenner's work, in Bronfenbrenner's system *"the person* exists in a system of relationships, roles, activities, and settings, all interconnected" (10). Part of that system, for military Brats, is the military itself, which impacts the individual, his or her parents (especially the service member), the individual's siblings and extended family, and the community in which the individual lives.

The environment in which a person develops, which Bronfenbrenner calls "develecological," is reciprocal and changing and can be either facilitating or harmful to the development of the child. Shelton suggests that too many transitions, identified as "[m]arriage, moving into a new home, birth of a child, sending a child off to elementary school, the onset of puberty, divorce, remarriage, and all the other many changes that take place across life" (118), can be harmful to development, especially if change is frequent, as it is in the life of the military child. This can lead to "adaptation overload," as Shelton calls it, which "might have undesirable effects on the person both physiologically and by depressing the person's motivation to explore and maintain the ecosystem or to engage in relationships in new settings" (54). That is, too many changes in a child's life can lead to stress that

## Five. "A Secure Base"

may cause the child to withdraw emotionally from those around him, which can affect his or her ability to develop and then sustain relationships. Life as a Military Brat is the very definition of "adaptation overload." Young children are expected to move at a moment's notice and to attend multiple schools during their childhoods. They fear the death or injury of their service member parent (or parents) multiple times, lose friends, sever or strain connections with extended families, and experience—multiple times—the loss of homes and pets that give the child a sense of place, identity and security.

John Bowlby agrees. In *A Secure Base* (1988), Bowlby says, "healthy, happy, and self-reliant adolescents and young adults are products of stable homes in which both parents give a great deal to time and attention to the children" (2). Stability and attention are thus key to secure attachment in childhood. This is, of course, difficult to impossible in many homes, but it is especially challenging in military households, where the extended absences of one parent are standard practice and attention is often fixed on the service member and his safety.

Bowlby's definition of successful parenting is "the provision by both parents of a secure base from which a child or an adolescent can make sorties into the outside world and to which he can return knowing for sure that he will be welcomed when he gets there, nourished physically and emotionally, comforted if distressed, reassured if frightened" (11). That "secure base," which is so important to Bowlby that it forms the title of his book, is nearly impossible with the military family, at least as it involves both parents, and it is frequently difficult even when one parent is holding down the "home front" and dealing with her own stressors such as fear, resentment, and the stress of parenting alone. As the word "sortie" in the previous quote suggests, Bowlby likens the ideal family to that of a military base "from which an expeditionary force sets out and to which it can retreat, should it meet with a setback. Much of the time the role of the base is a waiting one but is none the less vital for that. For it is only when the officer commanding the expeditionary force is confident his base is secure that he dares press forward and take risks" (11). What might be true for a military expedition is, unfortunately, not the case in the military

## Brat Life

family. While the actual base might be secured with armed guards and gates, the family base is precarious at best. Ironically, the children of the Fortress do not have such a fortress surrounding their family lives. They do not know where they will be living from one day to the next, and they do not know whether their parents will be returning from wherever they have mysteriously been sent. The military parent comes back to the base knowing that it will be secure, but the children living in the base have no such security.

Lacking such firm foundations, according to Bowlby, can "create intense anxiety but they also arouse anger, often also of intense degree, especially in older children and adolescents. This anger, the function which is to dissuade the attachment figure from carrying out the threat, can easily become dysfunctional" (30). As most Military Brats realize, anger at the system that is moving them around all the time and causing a parent to disappear from their lives is pointless, and they often turn that anger on themselves or deny it altogether. Thus, many Military Brats fall into what Bowlby calls "anxious avoidant attachment," when the child "tries to become emotionally self-sufficient and may be diagnosed as narcissistic" (124). As the comments of Military Brats in the previous chapters have shown, many children born into the Fortress may feel responsible for things—like war, death, absence, family cohesion—that they cannot control. They may also withdraw from all connection with friends and family, feeling uncertain about the permanence of any human interactions.

Bowlby continues that feelings of rejection, mistrust and/or withdrawal "occur especially in those who, having developed an anxiously avoidant pattern of attachment during early years, have striven ever since to be emotionally self-contained and insulated against intimate contacts with other people" (143). The child who realizes that she or he cannot depend on parents for a secure base translates those anxieties into emotional distance and lack of connection to others. It is possible to identify the "anxious avoidant attachment" in many military Brats. Having moved every few years, not knowing whether family members will return from deployments, not trusting that the family member at home will be able to cope, and not having stable attachments outside the family, Brats develop this coping style and appear to others as

## Five. "A Secure Base"

"resilient," which may be another word for emotionally detached. This resilience comes at a price. As Mary Wertsch has pointed out in her book, Brats often have difficulty making lasting friendships and feel cut off from the nonmilitary world when they enter it as adults. They also lose the capacity to feel the loss of these connections, to acknowledge what has been taken from them.

The famous Brats discussed here, while perhaps not entirely representative of the Brat experience, nonetheless show signs of this sort of avoidant attachment style, with a variety of consequences. While it might seem strange to lump L. Ron Hubbard, Jim Morrison, Newt Gingrich, and Suzanne Collins into a single analysis, they were all Military Brats, and some of the behaviors that manifest in their adult lives can be linked to their childhood experiences inside the Fortress. Whether the Brat becomes a science fiction writer and cult leader, a gifted rock star dead too early, a politician who shaped the political landscape of the 1980s and beyond, or an author of wildly popular young adult novels, the legacy of life in the Fortress has made an impact on their relationships, actions, and beliefs about the world.

L. Ron Hubbard (1911–1986), the Founder of Scientology—a combination of science fiction, pseudo-science, and religion, and eventually a paranoid and sometimes dangerous cult—was the son of a U.S. Naval officer. In his unauthorized biography of Hubbard, *Bare-Faced Messiah* (2018), critically respected author Russell Miller quotes a former member of Scientology as saying that Hubbard was "a mixture of Adolf Hitler, Charlie Chaplin and Baron Munchausen. In short, he was a con man" (Preface). Certainly, throughout his dramatic and self-aggrandizing life, he was a larger-than-life figure who was part prolific science fiction writer, part charlatan, part failed Naval officer, part religious leader, and part "commander" of a small fleet of run-down vessels from which he directed his increasingly paranoid and dangerous cult. However, as Lawrence Wright, biographer and chronicler of the Scientology movement, says in *Going Clear* (2013), "To label him a pure fraud is to ignore the complex, charming, delusional, and visionary features of his character that made him so compelling to the many thousands who followed him and the millions who read his work" (24). To make things even more complicated, as Miller says,

## Brat Life

"every biography of Hubbard published by the church [and there are many] is interwoven with lies, half-truths and ludicrous embellishments" (Introduction). In other words, it is often difficult to discover just who the real L. Ron Hubbard is, if there ever was a "real" person underneath the grandiose (and mostly false) life narrative.

The connections between the life that Hubbard manufactured (adventurous escapades, dramatic intellectual breakthroughs, and groundbreaking spiritual insights) and his background as a Military Brat can seem murky. Certainly, it has parallels with the much shorter but equally dramatic and self-destructive life of Jim Morrison, who was also the son of a Naval officer. As with Morrison, Hubbard resisted the authority of his military father and eventually cut himself off from his family, and, like Morrison, he struggled with personal relationships and substance abuse. How much of this is connected to their lives as Military Brats will be difficult to prove, but it is possible that the disconnections that Bowlby and Bronfenbrenner explore may in some small measure help to explain the motivations and the choices these two men made.

Initially, Hubbard's early life seemed relatively stable, as he stayed with his mother's family while his father was serving in World War I. If he "experienced any sense of loss from the absence of his father, it was certainly alleviated by the intense warmth and sociability of the Waterbury family [his maternal grandparents]," Miller says (24). However, after the war, his father (who was known as "Hub") wanted his wife May "to conform, like other Navy wives, and trail around the country with him from posting to posting," and "when he was at sea, he wanted her to be close to his ship's home port" (27). So, while May wanted to be with her husband, she worried about moving Ron frequently and being away from her parents, as she should have, given what other Military Brats have experienced. However, when Hub was posted to the battleship USS *Oklahoma* as an Assistant Supply Officer in 1921, the family moved to San Diego, the *Oklahoma*'s home port (27). At this point, Ron begins his life as a itinerate, disconnected Military Brat. In another interesting connection to Morrison, Wright notes that, like Morrison, "throughout his youth, he was fascinated by shamans and magicians" (25). In Hubbard's case, it may have been

## Five. "A Secure Base"

more of a desire to enhance an exotic self-narrative and less a desire to create a spiritual foundation for his work, but the origin of this fascination might have been the same: a desire for a supernatural continuity that did not exist in either of their itinerate lives.

Miller says that while Ron might have missed his maternal grandparents' home, "he did not appear to mind, in the least, being a 'Navy brat'—the curiously affectionate label applied to all children of servicemen, many of whom needed more than the fingers of both hands to count their schools. He was a gregarious boy, quick to make friends, and starting a new school held no terrors for him" (28). It appears that Ron fit the mold of the resilient and adaptable Brat. However, when his father was stationed in Guam and the family became concerned about the temptations that existed for young men there, his parents decided to send Ron back to Montana to live with his grandparents and finish high school (33). This attempt at creating stability in Ron's life failed. Like Morrison, Ron was not content to be abandoned with his grandparents, and he dropped out of high school and arranged to travel on a Navy ship to Guam. Although his mother and father were likely not happy about this rash decision, his parents allowed Ron to stay in Guam and study for his admission to the Naval Academy, which both Ron and his father wanted (44).

Despite being tutored by his mother, Ron failed the entrance examination to the Naval Academy and consequently attended a prep school for Academy candidates (48). However, as Miller says, Hubbard's father soon had to abandon his "heartfelt hope" that his son would attend the U.S. Naval Academy, as in his first semester at prep school, tests revealed him "to be so short-sighted that he stood no chance of passing the medical requirements for entry to Annapolis" (49). Clearly, Ron was not going graduate from the Naval Academy, and his subsequent attempt to matriculate at George Washington University ended when he dropped out after his second year (and nearly failing grades) (Miller 60). Clearly, as the son of a military officer, Ron was expected to follow in his father's footsteps or risk permanent estrangement from his father.

Despite being unable to secure admission to the Naval Academy or to finish college, Ron was commissioned as a Lieutenant (Junior

## Brat Life

Grade) in the U.S. Naval Reserve in advance of U.S. involvement in World War II (Miller 97). However, his father remained disappointed in him, which continued throughout both of their lives. A "a deeply conservative, utterly conventional plodder, a man ruled by routine and conformity," Hubbard's father couldn't accept his son's "refusal to get a job, his habit of staying up all night and sleeping all day, his prolonged absences from home, his lack of regard for his family" (Miller 99). Even though Ron had made it into the Navy, although with a special wartime appointment, his father remained disappointed in and often bewildered by his son. This may be due in part to his son's less-than-stellar Navy "career." Although he briefly commanded two ships during World War II, the Navy determined he was unfit for command both times. At one point during his brief command of a "sub chaser," Hubbard claimed to have bombed an enemy submarine during his time in the service, but this was determined to be an error. He spent the last months of his time in the Navy in the hospital for various ailments. This is clearly not the story that a Naval officer wants told about his son.

The feeling of disconnection and bewilderment was mutual. As Miller says, Ron "had nothing in common with his father who had spent virtually his entire life pushing paper in the Navy with nothing but the prospect of a pension" (99). Although most of L. Ron Hubbard's "adventures" would be fictional, he could not connect to a father who, while frequently being absent from his life, seemed to have little vision and less drive. Later, he told a friend and sometime lover that "his father was some sort of conman, a very shadowy kind of character, who he suspected was trying to take over Dianetics" (Miller 195). The distant and unfathomable father became, later in Ron's life, a threat to his son's elaborate fantasy life.

As for the women in his life, the best one can say is that it was complicated. Hubbard's first wife Polly refused to move to his Naval duty stations, having "a nightmare vision of trying to raise a family while trailing forlornly after her husband, backwards and forwards from one coast to another" (126). Given the stories of Brats discussed in previous chapters, this is a reasonable decision, yet her absence may have led, in part, to Hubbard's increasing number of infidelities and

## Five. "A Secure Base"

their eventual divorce. However, the disrespect he showed all his wives may have been part of a deeper misogyny, perhaps gleaned, in part, from the androcentric military world passed down from his father. *Dianetics*, the bible of the Scientology movement, in which Hubbard explored solutions to a wide range of psychological problems, "exposed a deep-rooted hatred of women, exemplified by a prurient pre-occupation with 'attempted abortions'" (Miller 156).

Hubbard's second wife, Barbara, said he told her "grotesque tales about his family mostly and his hatred of his mother, who he said was a lesbian and a whore.... He is a deeply unhappy man. He said the only thing to show him affection for the last few years, before he met me, was Calico, his cat" (169). In this comment, it is possible to see his avoidant attachment style. Given these animosities, it is not surprising that Hubbard had little contact with his parents, or the Waterbury family, after World War II. He visited his mother on the day of her death but did not stay for the funeral (237). As Wright says, "For a man as garrulous as L. Ron Hubbard turned out to be, reflections on his parents are rare, almost to the point of writing them out of his biography" (28). This disconnection to his family is similar to the ways Jim Morrison distanced himself from his mother and father, refusing to see them as an adult and writing them out of his life story.

In the midst of his rather chaotic personal life, Hubbard was writing science fiction at a prodigious pace and creating a new religion, outlined in his book *Dianetics*, which created the foundation for what would eventually become Scientology. This self-help, sci-fi, mental processing movement, which 2008 census data shows had 25,000 followers in the United States, has real-estate holdings in the billions of dollars and claims celebrity members such as Tom Cruise and John Travolta. According to their website, Scientology is "a religion that offers a precise path leading to a complete and certain understanding of one's true spiritual nature and one's relationship to self, family, groups, Mankind, all life forms, the material universe, the spiritual universe, the supreme being" (https://www.scientology.org/). It is interesting that this new religion is focused on both mastering the self and relationships with other people, given the interpersonal connections that seemed to have been missing in Hubbard's life with family,

## Brat Life

spouses, children, and others. Bowlby and Bronfenbrenner would have a field day with this statement.

In perhaps one of the most bizarre incidents in Hubbard's chaotic and eccentric life, in 1967 he "raised a private navy, appointed himself Commodore, donned a dashing uniform of his own design and set forth on an extraordinary odyssey, leading a fleet of ships across the oceans variously pursued by the CIA, the FBI, and international press and a miscellany of suspicious government and maritime agencies" (Miller 263). He referred to this group of run-down and refurbished ships and crew as "Sea Org," and life on the high seas protected him from imagined persecution and likely prosecution for his various financial schemes. Both Hubbard and Mary Sue, his third wife, who enjoyed their authority, "peppered their memoranda with military terminology and intelligence jargon" (Miller 297). Perhaps in keeping with his self-created image as a Naval officer, Ron "applied to the US Navy for the war medals he had always claimed he had been awarded but knew he had never won" (322). The Navy denied the application. Clearly, Hubbard was searching for ways to fulfill his father's dreams of military service for his son (without having to actually serve extended time in the real Navy).

While he was playing the role of "commodore," Ron received his father on board one of his "fleet." Hub "was eighty-eight years old and very frail, but determined to make peace with his estranged son. The old gentleman arrived on the quayside in a taxi and the Commodore went down the gangway to meet him—the first time anyone had ever seen him leave the ship to welcome a visitor" (Miller 329). The visit went well, in part because his father was so old and because all evidence of Scientology had been removed from sight. Ron's father "sat talking with his son for hours and wandered amiably about the ship evincing very little curiosity about what was going on. With a plentiful supply of beer and a couple of fishing trips, he was content. When he got back home to Bremerton, he told Marnie, his sister-in-law, that he had had a 'wonderful trip.' He died a few months later" (329). One wonders if his father thought that perhaps his son had finally achieved the dream he had had for him and taken command of his own naval vessel.

## Five. "A Secure Base"

Hubbard ended his life with the same dramatic flourishes that he had cultivated his entire career: "On 19 January 1986, Scientologists around the world received their last message from L. Ron Hubbard. In Flag Order number 3879, headed 'The Sea Org and The Future,' he announced that he was promoting himself to the rank of Admiral. Alongside the proclamation, in a Scientology magazine, was a colour photograph of the grey-haired Commodore in his Sea Org peaked cap. He was grinning broadly, with a definite twinkle in his eyes. He had never looked more like Puck" (Miller 369). Finally, Hubbard had become the man his father wanted, at least in all superficial aspects: he was a (self-appointed) commander of a fleet of ships, his staff obeyed him absolutely, and, best of all, he no longer had to prove himself to his father. According to Wright, Hubbard's ashes were scattered in the Pacific (227), which seems a fitting tribute for a man who fought against and simultaneously recreated life as a Naval officer, albeit of his own personal Navy.

Using the lenses provided by Bronfenbrenner and Bowlby, it is possible to see the ways in which L. Ron Hubbard followed the pattern outlined by Military Brats with attachment disorders. He became estranged from his family when he did not follow the expectations established by his Navy father—that he have a successful career as a military officer. His relationships with women and with his children were fraught, he drank heavily and abused prescription medications, and he created a fictional world in which he was the center of wisdom and adoration. Perhaps most importantly, he created a quasi-religious organization that bilked its followers out of millions of dollars and harassed and intimidated former followers who chose to speak out against him. As a child, Hubbard had little control over his environment, and his family was often separated from grandparents and other relatives that might have given him a sense of stability and identity. This is not to say that all Military Brats grow up to be fantasists who create cults and imaginary navies, but it possible to see the desire for connection and security in many of Hubbard's actions.

Perhaps less damaging to the wider public than Hubbard, but more self-destructive, is The Doors lead singer Jim Morrison, who rose quickly to fame in the 1960s and who was dead of a possible drug and alcohol overdose by age 27. As Stephen Davis points out in the beginning of his massive, 473-page biography of Morrison, *Jim Morrison: Life, Death, Legend* (2004), "Anyone inquiring more than superficially into Jim Morrison's life immediately realizes that the story of his childhood is crucial to understanding what happened to him later" (5). The problem, though, for understanding the musician is that "Jim Morrison's troubled and problematic post–World War II childhood within the sheltered, close-knit world of military families has been one of his story's most closely guarded mysteries" (5). This is, in part, because his family has refused to speak to biographers or the media, but it is also because life inside the Fortress is hidden from public view. Miliary families often choose to keep their family secrets within the family to protect the service member's career while he or she is alive—and to protect the military after they are gone.

Jim's father, who entered the Naval Academy in the 1930s and who eventually became Admiral Steve Morrison, was captain of the USS *Bonhomme Richard* for much of Morrison's childhood, and Jim was born in 1943 "amid the greatest burst of military energy his country ever experienced" (Davis 7). On a rising career trajectory, Steve Morrison "moved his young family around with very little notice as he earned promotions and his assignments changed" (7). In addition, Steve's "duties required a high-level security clearance that specified that his work was never discussed at home" (7). As soon as he was born, then, Jim Morrison experienced the dislocations and absence—both physically and psychologically—of his father. A typical Brat, Morrison lived with secrecy, dislocation, and paternal absence.

This creates perfect conditions for the avoidant attachment style and corresponding negative behaviors Jim Morrison began to exhibit. Davis says, "Experts have long observed that some children of military families may be at risk for various social problems and psychological disorders.... Jimmy's family moved four times before he was four years old, and this lack of stability may have engendered a physical restlessness and a sense of profound alienation that stayed with Jim Morrison for the rest of his life" (11). Restlessness, isolation, and alienation are classic elements in the creation of an avoidant attachment style, just as they are classic elements in a Brat's childhood. In

## Five. "A Secure Base"

addition, Jim's father "had to put the navy ahead of his family," as is common for military parents. Also, his father "tended to bark orders at his children" (11). Treating children as little soldiers or sailors is common in Brat life, especially in the lives of children of commissioned or non-commissioned officers (high ranking enlisted men), as Pat Conroy's and other Military Brats fictional and real-life stories show.

Davis describes quite well the ways in which Jim Morrison could stand as a metaphor of the Military Brat, as a "poster child for the instability of military families. The lack of roots, the father's continual absence, the mother's uneven discipline, the difficulties that a bright but socially isolated child encountered in receiving approval from friends, teachers, and parents, all can be used to explain Jim's urges to rebel in order to get the attention he needed" (12–13). While Davis notes that "some observers counter that these peripatetic military families form a larger, extended family that often provides a secure enclave for its own and produces flexible, well-adjusted children" (13), this idea of an "larger, extended family" that the military provides for Brats is, for the most part, illusory, especially after children start attending civilian high schools and age out of their Brathood by 18. Also, when Brats are younger, they are often at the mercy of a household whose authority is always shifting. For example, when Jim's father was able to spend more time at home after he rose in rank, "he reasserted his role in the family with a program of strict rules and discipline," which Jim and his brother resented (Davis 13).

Davis' biography deftly summarizes much of what was discussed earlier about attachment theory and shows its relationship to Jim Morrison's life story: attachment theory, he says, "suggests that children who receive insensitive, neglectful, or inconsistent care can develop difficulties with controlling their emotions, and often turn to drugs and alcohol to soothe themselves. Such children often have trouble with trusting other people and maintaining consistent relationships and may also become impossible to control" (13). "Insensitive, neglectful, or inconsistent care" are often the hallmarks of the military childhood. While not all of Jim Morrison's self-destructive behaviors can be directly traced to his time as a Military Brat, there does seem to be a correlation between these adverse childhood experiences and his subsequent rootlessness and substance abuse.

Jerry Hopkins and Danny Sugerman, who wrote *No One Here Gets Out Alive* (1995), another biography of Morrison, agree, saying that while "the negative aspects of rootlessness have been greatly overstated," some problems remain, especially for Navy Brats like Hubbard and Morrison, who come to realize "that even in peacetime there will be long periods when the father is aboard ship and, unlike land-based military people, he cannot take his dependents along. The family members learn to travel light, usually acquiring only essential items, such as furniture, silver, china, and linen. Jim and his brother and sister had toys and books, but not in abundance" (7). Hopkins and Sugerman add that while military parents may find camaraderie and community in the service members and spouses they meet at officers' and enlisted clubs on military bases, their children "generally find their friends in school, and navy children must find new ones more frequently" (7). The bottom line, Hopkins and Sugerman say, is that "the highly mobile society" of the military can lead to "a variety of emotional disorders, from alcoholism and marital discord to anomie and a sense of 'unconnectedness.' Probably the most significant factor is the periodic absence of the father. The mother's role repeatedly changes, depending on whether or not the father is home, and the children often suffer a confusion about and resentment of authority" (7–8). Again, the hallmarks of an attachment disorder are here: frequent moves, strife in the home, a disconnectedness from family and friends, and an uncertainty about who is in charge. Even when he was home, Hopkins and Sugerman say, Jim's father "was what he'd always been: mentally preoccupied or physically absent—visiting Cape Canaveral for the Vanguard space shots, playing golf at the Army-Navy Country Club, flying to keep his wings, and working mathematical puzzles at home rather than paying as much attention to Jim as Jim would have liked" (22). Jim's father did not seem interested in his children and spouse, and even his time at home was focused on what might help to advance his career. Rootlessness, disconnection, an absent father, and inconsistent discipline all contribute to a child's lack of attachment and connection, and also to the potential for substance abuse and mental illness.

## Five. "A Secure Base"

James Riordan and Jerry Prochnicky, writing in what the *New York Times* has said is "the most objective, thorough and professional Morrison biography yet," *Break on Through: The Life and Death of Jim Morrison* (1991), argue that "the rigid and intense mentality of the navy way and the almost continuous relocations of the family," along with "the male authority figure's absence for long periods of time," may have led to Jim's rebellion, which he achieved "both with enthusiasm and imagination" (28). This rebellion is consistent with what Bowlby and Bronfenbrenner have identified as the avoidant attachment style. While Jim learned to make friends quickly, the authors say, he also "learned not to get too close. He was afraid to open himself up to people, preferring to draw further into his mind and the security of his books because they were the things that couldn't be taken away from him" (31). This, too, is typical of attachment disorder issues and is par for the course in Brat life. Isolation, rebellion, and fear of failure resulting from unrealistically high standards all contributed to the troubled young man Jim Morrison became.

Even when Jim's father was home from deployment, problems arose as Steve tried to take over the role of disciplinarian, which his sons resented (29). Overall, Riordan and Prochnicky say, "While the captain could be a charmer in public, friends of the family say he fluctuated between treating his children as if they were green recruits or, worse, just leaving it all up to Clara. He was absent so often that he was almost a visitor to the household during his son's early life and he exercised little parental authority when he was there. As a result, Morrison's life would always lack personal discipline" (28). Again, correlation is not causation, but inconsistent discipline in the Morrison household must have left Jim, at the very least, confused. When their father was home, the Morrison children were expected to be perfect recruits, or they were left with little or no supervision from their mother, as she, too, struggled to cope with Steve's absences.

When Steve Morrison returned home for an extended period in 1960, Davis comments, "The tension in the household between the brusque, somewhat preoccupied officer and the renegade teenaged beatnik may have been unbearable" (25). Jim was also put off by his father's commanding presence onboard his ship, and he was reluctant

## Brat Life

to visit him there. "More than ever," Riordan and Prochnicky say, in Morrison's high school years, he "grew to hate conformity and authority. He was breaking loose, and Captain Morrison would never be able to regain touch with his son" (33). Over his high school years, Riordan and Prochnicky say, Jim had increasingly less respect for his father, "whom he felt had the power of a navy captain yet could not master his own household" (37). This story resonates with both Pat Conroy's and L. Ron Hubbard's childhoods, as it does with the stories of many Brats in this book.

Also echoing the experience of Hubbard, Jim's parents decided that he would live with grandparents in Florida for college while the family moved on to Coronado, near San Diego, for their next duty station (Davis 26). Like Hubbard as well, Morrison set out on his own to rejoin his family on the West Coast. After Morrison hitchhiked out to California in 1963, his mother would not let him in the house until he got a haircut. His father arrived home, and Jim met the ship. A friend told Davis that after a two-year separation, father and son "greeted each other with genuine affection" (41). However, this rapprochement was not to last. Davis says that although Jim dressed conservatively (for him) to visit his father onboard ship, "Captain Morrison took one look at his truculent, slouching son—aspiring Beat poet, Nouvelle Vague film buff, slacker collegiate draft dodger—and ordered him to the ship's barber for another, more military trim" (Davis 47). It is impossible to overestimate the importance of appearance for the military family. If children do not appear to conform, the leadership of the military father is suspect.

Ordering his son to have his hair cut suggests just one of the ways in which Steve treated Jim more like a recruit than a son. "Back in the San Diego area, Jim and Andy [Jim's brother] often went to movie theaters on post and sometimes Jim would sneak in wine and get drunk. On military bases a film of the flag is routinely shown after [actually before] the feature and the national anthem is played. Once Jim filled the theater with his voice.... He was the only one singing" (Hopkins and Sugerman 43). At this point, a high school Jim Morrison had decided to challenge the authority and the customs of Brat life. This would have been shockingly disrespectful behavior at what other Brats—real and fictional—describe as a formative event of their lives inside the Fortress. In outward appearance and behavior, Brats are expected to conform to the respect for the signs and symbols of American military life.

Although his father has said that he had never pressured his children to go into the Navy, "apparently the pressure of the navy life still ate away at Jim Morrison. Part of him was striking back at his parents by breaking away totally from their environment" (Riordan and Prochnicky 51). Jim's permanent move to the West Coast constituted that final break. This would have been a geographic break, but it also would have been a psychological break. Jim was signaling to his father that, whatever he might do with his life, it would not involve the military.

Not much is known for certain about what exactly caused this final and irrevocable estrangement between Jim and his parents, but after December 1964, Jim Morrison never saw his parents again (Davis 56). They also quit financing his lifestyle, and after he moved out of his parentally-supported California apartment, Jim Morrison "would never again have a home of his own" (Davis 72). A friend of Jim's told Davis that "Jim preferred motels. He chose motels for their neon signs. He would just disappear. He was like a Zen monk. No possessions. Had a credit card and a frayed driver's license in his pockets—nothing else" (338). Life with few possessions and living in motels mimics the transitory living conditions of the Military Brat. A generic motel room mimics the temporary quarters military families occupy, and they learn early on not to take too much stock in possessions.

At one point after he separated from his parents for good, Jim wrote to his father that he planned to start a band, which his father said sounded like "a crock," and which subsequently ended all father/son communication (Davis 79). Jim often said his parents were dead, and he told a bandmate that his father "ran the house like he ran his ship" (79). According to Riordan and Prochnicky, "Steve Morrison at age forty-seven had become the youngest admiral in the navy and was assigned to the Pentagon, moving the family to Arlington. It wasn't until well after the release of the first album that Steve and Clara became aware of their son's new career. To them Jim had long since disappeared into L.A.'s 'beatnik' underground" (163).

## Brat Life

At this point in his life, Davis says, Jim Morrison was "an amalgam of different personae, often shifting, dependent on the stimuli provided by the people he hung around with" (122). This is typical of the Military Brat, as the various fictional and nonfictional accounts of Brat life recounted in this book show. Conditioned by frequent moves, new schools, and an ever-shifting array of temporary friends, Brats learn to adapt quickly to the moods and preferences of those around them. It was around this time that Jim created "his new and obscene Oedipal mantra," which he incorporated into his song "The End" (131), which included lyrics about killing his father and sleeping with his mother. Jim's younger brother, Andy, would later say that their father, Admiral Morrison, showed no overt emotion when Andy played him his firstborn son's Oedipal ravings for the first time (Davis 196). When Andy played The Doors' first album for his parents, "Clara actually seemed to like most of it, but the commander sat hidden by his newspaper, pretending not to listen. When the Oedipal section of 'The End' came on, the newspaper began to shake as if with trembling or rage and kept shaking until the completion of the song. But the elder Mr. Morrison didn't say a word and has never once publicly commented on his son's career" (Riordan and Prochnicky 163). Military families are not likely to have conversations—between themselves or with others—about such dark angers and longings.

In addition to being caught in an Oedipal triangle, Jim Morrison was also haunted by the Vietnam War. Jim dreamed about napalm, which caused him insomnia (Davis 159), and yet he was "extremely interested when an Elektra promo man mentioned to him that the American military had ordered an unusually large shipment of *The Doors*, to be sold at the post exchanges in Vietnam. It was a signal of the future" (163). Always the military Brat, regardless of how he tried to escape it, Jim likely held fond memories of looking for records at post exchanges himself. However, having a father involved in a war that he found horrifying must have taken a toll on Jim's sense of right and wrong and increased the estrangement between himself and his parents.

During this time, Morrison told a roadie that he never wanted to talk to his mother again, and when Clara wanted to come backstage

## Five. "A Secure Base"

during the Washington, D.C., concert, "she was continually diverted and discouraged. Morrison never saw or spoke to her again. Money and power now ensured that his world didn't include anything in it he didn't want. And, among other things, that meant his parents" (Riordan and Prochnicky 163–64). Once he became famous and wealthy, Jim no longer had to placate his parents and could complete the estrangement that began in his early years.

Jim Morrison's meteoric rise and precipitous fall is well known to many. His self-destructive relationships with people, his suicidal abuse of drugs and alcohol, his peripatetic lifestyle, and his unpredictable moods are legendary. His musical legacy, however, remains intact decades after his untimely and somewhat mysterious death at 27. Jim's father was silent when he heard of his son's death, although he called the American Embassy in Paris for confirmation (Riordan and Prochnicky 456). The break between Jim Morrison and his parents had never been healed. It may not be possible to conclusively connect Morrison's life as a Navy Brat to what followed in his adult life, but, as with L. Ron Hubbard, his isolation and self-destructive behavior seemed linked to his military childhood. There is no question that his musical genius and commanding stage presence (when he was not falling-down drunk) have turned him into a cult figure in the music world, but his childhood as Military Brat may have been what was most formative in his life.

Although quite different from the cult leader and the rock star, Newt Gingrich, speaker of the U.S. House of Representatives from 1995 to 1999, prolific author, and self-appointed spokesperson for the new conservative movement in American politics, was another military child. As Craig Shirley, Gingrich's authorized biographer, says, Gingrich was adopted at eight by a career Army officer ("Introduction," xxiv). While Shirley calls Gingrich an "atypical army brat," as his stepfather and not his father, with whom he spent summers, was in the military, he was nevertheless often "a newcomer at school, once having to defend himself with his fists against boys challenging the new kid on the block. He'd lived on a half dozen different military bases as a child, including ones in France and Germany. While in France, he visited a macabre World War I memorial as a child,

## Brat Life

which had a lifetime effect on him" ("Introduction," xxiv). Moving frequently, being surrounded by the devastating effects of war, and living away from extended family, Gingrich in many ways had a typical Brat experience.

Although Gingrich has said he had "an idyllic childhood," Shirley notes that "when moving from his father's post in Kansas, the young Gingrich discovered to his horror that his box filled with his favorite toys—airplanes, fossils, books, and other things that delight the young, intellectual, if sometimes lonely, boy—had been lost in shipment. Little Newt was devastated for a time, but thereafter learned not to like things too much." Learning "not to like things too much" is typical of the insecure avoidant attachment style, as is the narcissism associated with Gingrich's later public personality. It is also part and parcel of the Brat experience. In addition, although Gingrich "hadn't grown up friendless, but moving year after year, the nearsighted kid found joy and happiness in books" (Shirley xxv). Books are a convenient source of comfort for Brats who are too often taken away from friends, schools, and activities. They are portable, easily moved from station to station, and the fictional depictions of secure families and readily-expressed emotions are a balm to connection-hungry Brats.

This bookish, lonely, disconnected child grows up to be a college professor, a congressman, the speaker of the U.S. House of Representatives, and *Time* magazine's Man of the Year in 1995. He helps to reshape the conservative movement during the Reagan years and beyond. Is it possible to link his views on welfare reform and capital gains, which punished the poor and benefited the wealthy, with his military upbringing? He avoided service in Vietnam, getting deferments for being a student and father, although he has said that he believed that he should have served. Married three times, he seemed to have a romantic life that rivaled that of L. Ron Hubbard, abandoning his first wife while she recovered from uterine cancer and his second wife when she was diagnosed with multiple sclerosis. Despite these aspects of his personal life, he vigorously pursued the impeachment trial of Bill Clinton for lying about his marital infidelities. Charismatic, with a zealot's enthusiasm and a confidence that he is in the right, Gingrich resembles L. Ron Hubbard. Unable to commit to a

## Five. "A Secure Base"

lasting relationship, he resembles Jim Morrison. Perhaps his creation of the new conservative movement in American politics, with its emphasis on patriotism and support of the military, may be a way for Gingrich to be the son a military officer expects.

For Suzanne Collins, the youngest of the famous personalities described here and author of the Hunger Games trilogy, it is difficult to pinpoint, as Laurie Adams puts it, "the precise moment when a little girl with an absent father came to the stunned understanding of the concept of war and the wrenching knowledge that a beloved parent was in the midst of this terrible danger" (17). However, the youngest daughter of U.S. Air Force Lieutenant Colonel Michael Collins and his wife, Jane Brady Collins, "has noted some of her first memories were of drills being conducted on the parade grounds of West Point" (Henthorne 13). According to Adams, Collins' father "taught at the Army's military academy only briefly, but his career and his intense interest in history, which was shared with his children at every opportunity, left a series of profound imprints on young Suzanne that would one day surface in her writing" (17).

In 1968, Collins' father was deployed to Vietnam. As Adams says, "Collins recounted the progression of fear that characterized that period in her life in her 2013 children's book *The Year of the Jungle*. First, there was the lack of understanding of why her father had to be away, accompanied by the anxiety that her mother would somehow vanish as well" (17–18). In *The Year of the Jungle*, cheerful illustrations by James Proimos are included with text that both chronicles ordinary childhood events and the very real worry first-grade Suzy has about her father's year in the jungle. When she hears about her father's deployment in Vietnam, Suzy's initial response is confusion and then pleasure when she associates the jungle to which her father will be sent with her favorite cartoon elephant, who also lives in a jungle. After her father deploys, Suzy receives postcards from him that ask about her school and admonish her to take care of the cat. At one point, though, her father asks her to "pray for me," which worries Suzy. She also notices strange reactions from adults when she tells them her father is in Vietnam. They seem "sad or worried or angry," which causes Suzy to worry as well. At one point, her father mixes up the birthdays of his children, and Suzy says, "The jungle must be a very confusing place for him to make such a serious mistake." As her concerns and confusion mount, the illustrations of jungle turn from smiling elephants and hippos to scenes of war and injury.

At one point, Suzy is watching television, on which the Vietnam War was covered extensively, and her mother "runs across the living room and turns off the TV." While she reassures Suzy that her father is okay, Suzy's response is to "hide in the closet and cry." As she moves into summer, Suzy feels that "so many things are scary now" and worries that her father will not make it home. "A year is long," she says poignantly. Eventually her father returns, but he is "different. Tired and thin and his skin has turned the color of pancake syrup." In addition, her father "stares into space." "He is here and not here," she says. "He is back in the jungle." As Adams says, "Collins' father returned from the war safely, but not unscathed, as he suffered recurrent nightmares" (18). Unable to express her own worries, Suzy displaces them onto their cat, Rascal. Her father reassures the cat that he is "home now." The book ends on a happy note, returning to the beginning reference to Ogden Nash and a dragon named Custard who "is really the bravest of all."

Throughout the book, Suzy is faced with concerns that most people in her environment do not share and those who do, do not want to talk about it. She prides herself on being the "bravest" of all, but readers see throughout the book the ways in which the war and her father's absence have infiltrated her psyche. This is a nearly-universal Brat experience. Forces beyond your scope of awareness and certainly beyond your control are swirling about your life, and there is nothing you can do about it other than "hide in the closet and cry" and hope that your father, who has returned physically, will also return psychologically from the war. Unfortunately, this is rarely the case: PTSD from combat experiences blights the lives of both the service member and his family for years to come.

In addition to shaping Collins' young life and psyche with his absence, Collins' father "made a point of teaching his children to trace the underlying causes of wars and question their necessity, imbuing his lessons with grim reality" (18). Like Gingrich in front of the war

## Five. "A Secure Base"

memorial in France, Jim Morrison on his father's warship, and L. Ron Hubbard travelling to Guam to visit his family, Collins and other military Brats learn early on the human cost of war and the dangers into which their parents willingly go. As Adams says, "Throughout her young life, by chance exposure, nurturing, and her own choices, Collins' voice as a writer was being shaped to examine how people live, how people die, and how the stories of those events should be told" (19).

Not surprisingly, then, from the beginning of the Hunger Games series "Collins depicted characters whose lives allowed her to express the full scope of the emotional impact of war on both her father as an adult combatant and her former six-year-old self as a helpless spectator" (Adams 20). In this series, she chronicles the "despair of home-front families helplessly watching warzone media coverage" (21). Collins wanted, Adams says, "to challenge what she believed was the growing risk of desensitization of the media-consuming population to images of warfare in an age of blurring lines between information and entertainment" (21). She also "felt her other goal was to address the concept of war and its costs to children at all reading levels" (21). Collins told *Time* magazine that if she "took the 40 years of my dad talking to me about war and battles and taking me to battlefields and distilled it down to one question, it would be the idea of the necessary or unnecessary war" (21). This question about war has haunted all the Brat stories described in this study. Although they are not combatants themselves, they have experienced firsthand the costs of war.

In "Suzanne Collins's War Stories for Kids," the *New York Times* (2011), Susan Dominus says that "although young-adult fiction often dispenses with caretakers to give the characters control over their own lives, the anxiety provoked by an absent parent seems particularly pivotal in Collins's fiction" (NP). This may be an important distinction. Whereas in much YA fiction the absent parent frees up the adolescent for adventures, fiction written by Brats is often fraught with the very real fear that a parent might not be there when he or she returns from those escapades. Dominus continues: "The lifelong repercussions of Collins's father's service in Vietnam also provided her with a perspective that fuels a key plot twist of 'Mockingjay,' which follows one character's struggle to recover from tortured memories of violence..." (NP). Collins imbues her characters with the values of self-sacrifice and bravery and saddles them with traumatic memories of their parents' absences or deaths. Perhaps most importantly for the connections made in this study between Brat childhoods and their later lives, "Collins's heroes are, if anything, models of responsibility" (NP). Forced into adult roles and asked to repress their emotions for a larger good, military Brats like Collins learn early to pretend to be brave, even if they are not sure that they can be.

Despite the similarities outlined here, L. Ron Hubbard, Jim Morrison, Newt Gingrich, and Suzanne Collins can still seem an unlikely grouping. The founder of a religious cult and creator of his own Navy, a self-destructive rock singer, a Republican congressman and intellectual founder of the New Right in American politics, and a young adult novelist still seem to have very little in common, aside from their experiences as Military Brats. However, each of them experienced the rootlessness, frequent dislocations, inconsistent and absent parenting, and the rigorous attention to self-discipline attached to children who grow up inside the Fortress. Are there consistencies between the kinds of work they create? Can the proponent of Reaganomics, the creator of groundbreaking rock anthems, the author of a famous franchise of young adult novels and movies, and the founder of Scientology have anything in common? Would Pat Conroy or his fictional alter ego find himself at home with these fellow Brats?

It is possible to connect a longing for consistent and loving parenting, a desire to please, a fear of disappointment, and a constant sense of threat that may have informed the lives and psyches of these four individuals and the countless others examined in the fictional and nonfictional works presented in this study? Although some of what these men and woman have created is enduring and culturally rich—where would we be without "Riders on the Storm" or the Hunger Games series?—others have been damaging demagogues and troubled souls. On the surface, they seem to share little, but underneath one can see the haunting ghosts of life inside the Fortress. L. Ron Hubbard and Jim Morrison struggle their entire lives to please their Navy fathers; Newt

## Five. "A Secure Base"

Gingrich creates an entire political ideology that compensates for his lack of military service; and Suzanne Collins works out the trauma of her father's time in Vietnam through a series of heroic young adult characters. Each of these men and women never leave behind, no matter how hard they try, the tangled legacies of life inside the Fortress.

# Conclusion

## "Warriors [and Their Families] Have a Right to Reclaim Their Lives": The Price We Pay and the Solutions We Can (But Do Not) Offer

> Like it or not, the country is fighting on several fronts. Few have been asked to sacrifice anything for the war effort. Indeed, the only Americans who sacrifice are the members of our armed forces, their families, and friends.
> —J.G. Pryce, D.H. Pryce, and Shackleford, xi

In their 2016 book, *The Costs of Courage*, Josephine and David Pryce and Kimberly Shackleford document the crisis facing our country because of continued wars in Iraq and Afghanistan, as well as the continuing legacy of Vietnam. As they say, "The physical injuries of the wounded are horrific enough, but the huge costs of mental injury are just as daunting, and estimates hold that those unseen wounds will continue to increase, threatening the very survival of the veteran and his or her family" (xi). These warriors, they continue, have been used "until they are broken," and then hustled off to the overwhelmed and underfunded Department of Veterans Affairs (xii). The result, they argue, is a human crisis "of our own making" (xii). As this book has shown, those physically and psychologically-wounded veterans return home to families and extend the burdens to the people who love them and, eventually, to the country as a whole.

Shackleford and the Pryces also point out that deployments

## Conclusion

strain families who "fear for the soldier's safety, living conditions, and health. Family members become lonely and apprehensive about adapting to new and unfamiliar roles. Lack of or negative media reporting about the war effort creates even more stress" (26). These issues apply especially to the children of warriors. Once soldiers return, the physical wounds, as well as the PTSD, the depression, and the psychological effects of traumatic brain injury, may take "a lifetime of care giving, thus spawning increased incidences of domestic violence and divorce" (26). The military health community must find ways to deal with these combat stress injuries and, most importantly, ensure "that combat veterans do not feel dishonored by combat stress injuries" (34). The authors put it very well: "If we are going to send soldiers to the killing fields, we owe them the right to the knowledge of what the cost may be, and we must ensure them that transition and healing can follow. Warriors have a right to reclaim their lives" (81). Unless we are honest with service members and their families, these warriors (and the people who love them) will never "reclaim their lives." In addition, we need to focus on a smooth transition to life after deployment, whether that means transitioning to civilian life or continuing in the military. "Reclaiming their lives" also means integrating into family life again and learning how to be parents and spouses once more.

In addition, the families of service men and women need help transitioning from wartime to peacetime, from military life to civilian life. As Florence Kaslow says in *The Military Family in Peace and War* (1993), "The military has an ethical and existential responsibility to be mindful of the impact the service member's activities and whereabouts have on his/her parents, siblings, spouse, children, and grandparents" (xiii). This applies to the nonmilitary communities into which these service men and women return. Thus, we are all called upon, both philosophically and morally, to consider the needs of the families of those in the military. The Pryces and Shackleford concur: "Never before in American history has so much been asked of military family members and significant others" (119), and these military families have changed in recent decades to include more "single parents, dual-career couples, and women deployed to hazardous duty and assigned to combat units than ever before" (120). The complex needs

## Conclusion

of service men and women, both while in the military and when they leave it, are growing every day.

The good news is that there are far more resources for military families than ever before. The Army Community Services (ACS) and Morale, Welfare, and Recreation (MWR) were created in the 1980s after a white paper was published on the needs and pressures of military families (*The Costs of Courage* 123). Family Readiness Groups began in the 1980s to provide support for all spouses and families in a given military unit (130). In 2007, the Army committed $1.4 billion for family support programs (124). These are steps in the right direction, although problems still remain.

The situation is a good news/bad news one. Shackleford and the Pryces acknowledge that military life means that the service member has stable employment and opportunities for advancement; family members have access to free health care; housing is provided; vacations are authorized; and most bases where servicemen/women and their families are stationed have athletic and recreational facilities, non-taxed food and beverages, mental health services, and a wide variety of other support activities (128). However, challenges still include the stresses of living away from extended families, separations on the part of children from one or both parents, the threat of death or injury of the service member, long work hours, the need to conform to military expectations, life in foreign countries, and difficulties for spouses to find employment (129). Some of these issues are part and parcel of military life and may not be amenable to change, but others are responsive to various social and psychological interventions.

Additionally, the military is changing demographically, and therefore the needs of military spouses and Brats are changing as well. In *Strengthening the Military Family Readiness System* (2019), Kenneth W. Kizer and Suzanne Le Menestrel say that "today's service members may create new families that are more diverse or complex than in the past.... This rising diversity and complexity also could likely increase the difficulty of creating military policies, programs and practices that adequately support families in the performance of service members' military duties" (2). To summarize, families are different today, and they have complex and multivalent needs. In response, the DoD's

## Conclusion

Family Readiness policy "was overhauled in 2012, and policy makers have made major revisions to the military retirement, compensations, and benefits system. Other significant reorganization efforts include a consolidation of social support systems under the Defense Health System" (2).

Kizer and Le Menestrel also point out that "[f]amily resilience processes (e.g., effective communication strategies, emotional regulation, problem solving, and competent parenting) serve as opportunities for promotion, prevention, and intervention in the wake of stress and trauma" (8). The problem is that, despite information about support being available to military families, it remains unclear "the extent to which service providers at the various level of organization (DoD-wide, service branch, installation-based, and military-focused nonprofit) are aware of one another or can or do coordinate service provision" (11). Given the built-in mobility of military families, coordination of services across the network of military bases is crucial. It is also vital to extend those services outside of the military community and into the civilian world.

In his 2014 article, "School-Age Children of Military Families: Theoretical Applications, Skills Training, Considerations, and Interventions," Carlos V. Guzman says that "over the past several years, there has been substantial growth in the number of services offered to support military families" (9), like Families OverComing Under Stress (FOCUS), which "integrates evidence-based preventive interventions and adapts them to the needs of military families who are facing all phases of wartime deployments" (10). Guzman says that research suggests military adolescents, in particular, "feel most comfortable sharing with peers who understand these unique stressors as well as the military culture" (12). Clearly, the problem is being recognized and attempts at solutions are being undertaken.

Still, studying the children of the military can be difficult, Guzman acknowledges that "given the difficulty that civilians often face in obtaining approval to work with military families, treatment evaluations and development may be facilitated through collaboration between civilian and military personnel with expertise in treatment development, delivery, and dissemination work with youths and their

*Conclusion*

families" (13). Given the reflexive secrecy of the Fortress, for programs such as the ones discussed here to work, the military must collaborate with civilian therapists, social workers, and physicians. In their 2017 article, Shelly MacDermid Wadsworth, Keisha M. Bailey, and Elizabeth C. Coppola agree that studying military children is challenging because of incomplete records, military IRBs' reluctance to approve studies, and the difficulty in locating children whose parents have left the military. Also, those accepted into the military and those deployed may not be representative of the general population (26). Still, the authors acknowledge that while the parents' military service "exposes children to a variety of challenges, including relocation, separation, victimizations at school and the possibility that parents will be exposed to danger ... it also can provide children with benefits and opportunities, including access to health care, early childhood education, youth programs, and financial resources, at least while parents serve" (27). As has been pointed out earlier, military life has its advantages, especially when compared to the civilian population, but it also creates challenges that are usually not present in the nonmilitary world.

One solution for Brats may lie in recreational services. Haley K. Griffiths and Jasmine A. Townsend discuss the value of recreation-based camps for military children. In their 2018 article. Griffiths and Townsend argue that such camps "have seen a recent emergence as a nontraditional option for military families working through deployment and reintegration-related challenges" (100). These kinds of camps, the authors say, "may facilitate youth growth and development in areas such as self-awareness, independence, leadership, resilience, physical activity, social skills and social comfort, peer relationships, and environmental awareness" (100). Camps such as Camp Adventure, Military Teen Adventure Camps, Purple Camp, and Operation Military Kids provide "a unique and supportive environment for fostering positive youth outcomes, such as resilience, self-esteem, and a sense of belonging" (104). Camps such as these provide Brats with changes to share experiences and anxieties with peers who understand the unique lives that they lead.

In addition to recreational therapies for older children,

## Conclusion

interventions are needed for young Brats as well. Joy D. Osofsky and Lieutenant Colonel Malinda M. Chartrand say in their 2013 article that very young children, who like routine and are dependent on their parents, "may experience more stress than older children do when deployment and unexpected changes disrupt the family, and especially when changes and adjustments become part of family life" (62). They are at risk for child neglect and maltreatment on the part of spouses who suffer from a variety of psychological disorders resulting from deployment (65–66). The military's Family Advocacy Program, Osofsky and Chartrand say, "is designed to prevent partner violence, child abuse, and neglect by improving family functioning, easing the kinds of stress that can lead to abusive behavior, and working to create an environment that supports families" (70). In addition, the New Parent Support Program "helps military families with young children adapt to parenting" (70). Without a doubt, the military community is starting to pay attention to the needs of its children.

Other initiatives include a 2009 partnership between the military and ZTT (Zero to Three), the National Center for Infants, Toddlers, and Families, which resulted in the creation of Coming Together Around Military Families, which "offered specialized training and support for professionals and organizations that assist military families in and around military communities, with a focus on the stress of deployment" (70). Although the program no longer exists, many of the materials created are still available and could be used in similar programs in the future. In 2006, "the Sesame Workshop partnered with Wal-Mart to create Talk, Listen, Connect: Helping Families During Military Deployment, which includes a video, storybooks, and workbooks" (71), and Osofsky and Chartrand also argue for the value of Children-Parent Psychotherapy (71). The bottom line is that "we need to pay more attention to the needs of young children in military families" (72). They conclude that, for military families, "being in the military is not just a job, but a way of life. Clinicians and scientists who work with these families need to engage more fully in the process of developing and applying evidence-based knowledge to help ease the transitions that are part of military life and to support young children's resilience" (73). Given their particular needs, caused in part by

## Conclusion

the frequent dislocations and the unexpected and stressful changes that frequently occur in Brats' lives, Military-Brat-centered programs need to be created, maintained, and, most importantly, funded on an ongoing basis. Military bases already provide day care, swimming pools, gyms, and theaters for the children living there; it is a small but necessary step to provide adequate and destigmatized mental health care as well.

In a 2018 article on evidence-based interventions for military children's biopsychosocial needs, Alisa Hathaway, Justin Russotti, Jed Metzger, and Catherine Cerulli corroborated what other investigators have said: that military children suffer attachment disorders, PTSD, parentification, anger, resentment, and/or guilt as a result of deployment (55–57). However, barriers to care, they argue, include "lack of appropriate and accessible interventions," as well as "stigma and concerns regarding confidentiality ... and lack of professionals versed in working with the military population and family members" (57). Also, they note that the Veterans Administration is not designed for family-based services (57). Ultimately, the authors say, "there is no specific model for providing specialized mental health treatment for military children" (58). Clearly, camps are not enough: the specific issues that military children face have not been addressed; nor have their particular needs been met.

In addition, the authors say, "Many military children primarily function within a civilian culture (e.g., educational system) while also identifying with the military culture and the realities of active war" (65). Military children often "build a shield around themselves" in order to survive the strain (66). Generally: "Clinicians need to be mindful of their preconceived notions regarding military culture, war, and the men and women and families who serve our country" (71). Some of the bias the general population has toward the military is reflected in the attitudes some clinicians have toward service men and woman and their families. Finally, "Given the risk and sacrifice that deployment involves, the researchers want to emphasize the importance of incorporating the voices, needs, and recommendations of military personnel, their families, and affiliated community providers to tailor services to meet the unique needs of this population" (72).

## Conclusion

Indeed, military families should be consulted about what they *actually need* in terms of interventions and services.

All of this sounds good, although given the barriers to care that are part and parcel of military life—frequent relocations, the lack of adequate mental health services for service members and their families, the culture of secrecy that surrounds the military—these interventions may often be more theoretical than actual. Also, given the prevailing ethos of doing one's duty, refusing to acknowledge pain or weakness, and the need to protect the service member from retribution, providing social and psychological services for Brats and spouses will remain an uphill battle.

Perhaps this is where literature can come in. Works like the ones discussed in this book can provide Brats with a sense that they are not alone; that the fear, the loneliness, the pride, and the sense of sacrifice they feel are shared by others, both in the present and the past. As with veterans, Brats need to feel connected to those who know what they have experienced. Reading about Pat Conroy's conflicts and eventual reconciliation with his larger-than-life Marine pilot father, Elizabeth Berg's difficulties with her remote and unpredictable Army father, and Sarah Bird's struggle with her family's secrets, just to name a few, will likely resonate with Brats' own experiences. Young adult novels such as those by Daphne Benedis-Grab, Ashlee Cowles, Vicki Bohe-Thackwell, Frances O'Roark Dowell, Roseanne Parry, Sara Lewis Holmes, and Michael Joseph can help younger Brats realize that they are not alone—that others have experienced the pride, the fear, and the loss that they have. Autobiographies by Les Arbuckle, Sandy Hannah, Gail Hosking Gilberg, Ben and Anne Purcell, Louise Steinman, Diane Ryan, and Pat Conroy offer important insights for (mostly) former Brats who, as adults, are trying make sense of their lives and the lives of their military parents. Other works analyzing the Brat experience, especially Mary Edwards Wertsch's groundbreaking *Military Brats: Life Inside the Fortress*, can help Brats to make sense of the conflicting emotions they have about their childhoods and to feel less alone in the civilian world.

This population of nomads, of de facto service members who never enlisted or were drafted, who were born into a life that demanded

## Conclusion

sacrifice and precluded complaint, deserve a community after they are exiled from the Fortress. They may not have a hometown or many friends from childhood, but they do have a shared sense of both duty and burden, of pride and fear, of commitment and self-denial, and they may again find their tribe in the pages of these literary and analytical works. While the summer camps and mental health interventions can help, there is nothing like a shared sense of sacrifice and of honor, which is present on every page of the books discussed here. We have a duty of care for the children of warriors as much as we do for the warriors themselves, and it is my hope that this book will help Brats to know that they are not alone: others have shared their hopes, dreams, dislocations, fears, and devotion to duty. A book such as this one only recounts the joys and the terrors that accompany Brat life, but sometimes knowing that someone shared your battles is enough.

# Bibliography

Adams, Laurie. "Suzanne Collins: One Life, Three Acts, Scripted by War." *The Hunger Games Trilogy: Critical Insights.* Ed. Lana A. Whited. Ipswich, MA: Salem Press, 2016, 17–23. Book.
Barry, Michael. "Black Holes, Graveyards, and the Gravitational Force of What's Below: Mason's *In Country.*" *Papers on Language and Literature* 49, no. 2 (Spring 2013): 141–71. Ebsco.
Benedis-Grab, Daphne. *Army Brats.* New York: Scholastic, 2017. Book.
Berg, Elizabeth. *Durable Goods.* New York: Ballantine, 1995 (2004). Book.
_____. *Joy School.* New York: Ballantine, 1997 (1998). Book.
_____. *True to Form.* New York: Washington Square Press, 2002. Book.
Bird, Sarah. *The Yokota Officers Club.* New York: Ballantine, 2001 (2002). Book.
Bohe-Thackwell, Vicki. *Too Skinny to Float.* San Jose: Writers Club Press, 2000. Book.
Bowlby, John. *A Secure Base: Parent-Child Attachment and Healthy Human Development.* New York: Basic, 1988. Book.
Bronfenbrenner, Urie. *The Ecology of Human Development: Experiments by Nature and Design.* Cambridge: Harvard University Press, 1979. Book.
Cadden, Mike. "Genre as Nexus: The Novel for Children and Young Adults." *Handbook of Research on Children's and Young Adult Literature.* Eds. Shelby A. Wolf, Karen Coats, Patricia Enciso, and Christine A. Jenkins. New York: Routledge, 2011, 302–13. Book.
Clifton, Grace. "Making the Case for the BRAT (British Regiment Attached Traveler)." *British Educational Research Journal* 30, no. 3 (2004): 457–62. Ebsco.
_____ "The Origins of the Term 'Brat.'" https://static1.squarespace.com/static/544d9dc8e4b0489fb89d37c0/t/545984a2e4b0780b4 455c539/1415152802191/TheWordBrat.pdf. Website.
Collins, Carol Jones. "Finding the Way: Morality and Young Adult Literature." In Vandergrift, 157–83. Book.
Collins, Suzanne. *The Year of the Jungle.* Illustrated by James Proimos. New York: Scholastic Press, 2013. Kindle edition.
Conroy, Pat. *The Death of Santini: The Story of a Father and His Son.* New York: Dial Press, 2013 (2014). Book.
_____. *The Great Santini.* New York: Dial Press, 1976 (2013). Book.
Cowles, Ashlee. *Beneath Wandering Stars.* Blue Ash, OH: Merit Press, 2016. Book.

# Bibliography

Davis, Stephen. *Jim Morrison: Life, Death, Legend.* New York: Gotham, 2005 (2004). Book.
Dominus, Susan. "Suzanne Collins's War Stories for Kids." *The New York Times Magazine*, April 8, 2011. https://www.nytimes.com/2011/04/10/magazine/mag-10collins-t.html. Accessed 2/22/22. Website.
Douglas, Kate. *Contesting Childhood: Autobiography, Trauma, and Memory.* New Brunswick: Rutgers University Press, 2010. Book.
Dowell, Frances O'Roark. *Shooting the Moon.* New York: Atheneum, 2010. Book.
Ender, M.G., ed. *Military Brats and Other Global Nomads.* Westport, CT: Praeger, 2002. Book.
Gilberg, Gail Hosking. *Snake's Daughter: The Roads in and Out of War.* Iowa City: University of Iowa Press, 1997. Book.
Gilmore, Leigh. *The Limits of Autobiography: Trauma and Testimony.* Ithaca: Cornell University Press, 2001. Book.
Goode, Erich. *Justifiable Conduct: Self-Vindication in Memoir.* Philadelphia: Temple University Press, 2013. Book.
Griffiths, Haley K., and Jasmine A. Townsend. "Recreation-Based Camps for Military Children: Past, Present, and Future." *Journal of Outdoor Recreation, Education, and Leadership* 10, no. 2 (2018): 97–108. Ebsco.
Guzman, Carlos V. "School-Age Children of Military Families: Theoretical Applications, Skills Training, Considerations, and Interventions." *Children & Schools* 26, no. 1 (January 2014): 9–14. Ebsco.
Hanna, Sandy. *The Ignorance of Bliss: An American Kid in Saigon.* Brentwood, TN: Post Hill Press, 2019. Book.
Harrison, Deborah, and Patrizia Albanese. *Growing Up in Armyville: Canada's Military Families During the Afghanistan Mission.* Waterloo, Canada: Wilfrid Laurier University Press, 2016. Book.
Hathaway, Alisa, Justin Russotti, Jed Metzger, and Catherine Cerully. "Meeting Military Children's Biopsychosocial Needs: Exploring Evidence-Based Interventions." *Best Practices in Mental Health* 12, no. 1 (Spring 2018): 54–77. Ebsco.
Hinrichsen, Lisa. "'I can't believe it was really real': Violence, Vietnam, and Bringing the War Home in Bobbie Ann Mason's *In Country*." *Southern Literary Journal* 11, no. 2 (Spring 2008): 232–48. Ebsco.
Holmes, Sara Lewis. *Operation Yes.* New York: Arthur A. Levine, 2009. Book.
Hopkins, Jerry, and Danny Sugerman. *No One Here Gets Out Alive: The Biography of Jim Morrison.* New York: Grand Central, 2006 (1995). Book.
Jeffords, Susan. *The Remasculinization of America: Gender and the Vietnam War.* Bloomington: Indiana University Press, 1989. Book.
Johnson, Alison M. "Sam Hughes as a Second Generation Trauma Victim in Bobbie Ann Mason's *In Country*." *War, Literature, and the Arts*, January 1, 2014, 1–15. Ebsco.
Kaslow, Florence W. "Preface." *The Military Family in Peace and War.* New York: Springer, 1993. Book.
Kizer, Kenneth W., and Suzanne le Menestrel, eds. *Strengthening the Military Family Readiness System for a Changing American Society.* Washington, D.C.: National Academies Press, 2019. Book.
Lange, Katie. "'Military Brat': Do You Know Where the Term Comes From?" U.S. Department of Defense, April 12, 2017. https://www.defense.gov/Explore/Inside-

## Bibliography

DOD/Blog/Article/2060438/military-brat-do-you-know-where-the-term-comes-from/. Website.
Lyons, Michael Joseph. *Brat and the Kids of Warriors*. Chicago: Bravur Media, 2017. Book.
Mason, Bobbie Ann. *In Country*. New York: Harper & Row, 1985. Book.
_____. *Patchwork: A Bobbie Ann Mason Reader*. Lexington: University Press of Kentucky, 2018. Book.
Miller, Russell. *Bare-Faced Messiah: The True Story of L. Ron Hubbard*. London: Silvertail Books, 2014 (1987). Kindle edition.
Mountz, Thomas C. "Special Warriors, Special Families, and Special Concerns." *The Military Family in Peace and War*. Ed. Florence W. Kaslow. New York: Springer, 1993, 121–29. Book.
Murray, Gail Schmunk. *American Children's Literature and the Construction of Childhood*. New York: Twayne, 1998. Book.
Osofsky, Joy D., and Lieutenant Colonel Malinda M. Chartrand. "Military Children from Birth to Five Years." *The Future of Children* 23, no. 2 (Fall 2013): 61–77.
Parry, Roseanne. *Heart of a Shepherd*. New York: Random House, 2009. Book.
Pollack, Harriet. "From *Shiloh* to *In Country* to *Feather Crowns*: Bobbie Ann Mason, Women's History, and Southern Fiction." *The Southern Literary Journal* 28, no. 2 (Spring 1996): 95–116. Ebsco.
Price, Joanna. *Understanding Bobbie Ann Mason*. Columbia: University of South Carolina Press, 2000. Book.
Privitera, Charles R. "The Preschool Child and the Military Family." *Children of Military Families: A Part and Yet Apart*. Eds. Edna J. Hunter and D. Stephen Nice. Washington, D.C.: U.S. Government Printing Office, 1978, 5–7. Book.
Pryce, Josephine G., David H. Pryce, and Kimberly K. Shackelford. *The Costs of Courage: Combat Stress, Warriors, and Family Survival*. New York: Oxford University Press, 2016. Book.
Purcell, Ben, and Anne Purcell. *Love and Duty*. New York: St. Martin's, 1992. Book.
Regen, Richard. "Behind the Doors." Review of *Break on Through: The Life and Death of Jim Morrison*. *New York Times*, July 14, 1991. Ebsco.
Riordan, James, and Jerry Prochnicky. *Break on Through: The Life and Death of Jim Morrison*. New York: William Morrow, 1991. Book.
Schertz, Kelly, and Cassidy Watson. "What Becomes of America's Military Brats?" *AJPH* 108, no. 7 (July 2018): 837. Ebsco.
Seltzer, Catherine. *Understanding Pat Conroy*. Columbia: University of South Carolina Press, 2015. Book.
Shay, Jonathan. *Achilles in Vietnam: Combat Trauma and the Undoing of Character*. New York: Scribner's, 1994. Book.
Shelton, Lawrence G. *The Bronfenbrenner Primer: A Guide of Develecology*. New York: Routledge, 2019. Book.
Shirley, Craig. *Citizen Newt: The Making of a Reagan Conservative*. Nashville: Nelson Books, 2017. Book.
Sinor, Jennifer. "Inscribing Ordinary Trauma in the Dairy of a Military Child." *Biography* 26, no. 3 (2003): 405–27. Ebsco.
Steinman, Louise. *The Souvenir: A Daughter Discovers Her Father's War*. Berkeley: North Atlantic Books, 2001. Book.

# Bibliography

Tribunella, Eric. *Melancholia and Maturation: The Use of Trauma in American Children's Literature.* Knoxville: University of Tennessee Press, 2010. Book.

Trites, Robert Seelinger. "The Harry Potter Novels as a Test Case for Adolescent Literature." *Style* 35 (Fall 2001): 472–85. Project Muse.

Truscott, Mary R. *Children of the American Military Speak Out.* New York: Dutton, 1989. Book.

Vandergrift, Kay. "Introduction." *Mosaics of Meaning: Enhancing the Intellectual Life of Young Adults Through Story.* Ed. Kay Vandergrift. Lanham, MD: Scarecrow Press, 1996. Book.

Wadsworth, Shelly MacDermid, Keisha M. Bailey, and Elizabeth C. Coppola. "U.S. Military Children and the Wartime Deployments of Family Members. *Child Development Perspectives* 11, no. 1 (2017): 23–28. Ebsco.

Watson, Jay. *Reading for the Body: The Recalcitrant Materiality of Southern Fiction, 1893–1985.* Athens: University of Georgia Press, 2012. Book.

Wertsch, Mary Edwards. *Military Brats: Legacies of Childhood Inside the Fortress.* New York: Harmony, 1991. Book.

Wright, Lawrence. *Going Clear: Scientology, Hollywood, & the Prison of Belief.* New York: Vintage, 2013. Book.

York, Lamar. "Pat Conroy's Portrait of the Artist as a Young Southerner." *The Southern Literary Journal* 19, no. 2 (Spring 1987): 34–36. Project Muse.

# Index

Adams, Laurie 143–145
Afghanistan 4–5, 42, 46, 58, 66, 76, 78, 149
Albanese, Patrizia 45–47, 50–51
alcohol use 7, 13, 46, 69, 73, 84–85, 134–136, 141
Allingham, G.E. 12; *Growing Up in Khaki* 12
Arbuckle, Les 12, 20, 24, 44, 156; *Saigon Kids* 12, 20–25
*Army Brats* 12, 57, 62–66
attachment styles 6, 13, 61, 112, 125–127, 131, 133, 142, 155

Bailey, Kiesha M. 4–6, 153
*Base Jumping* 12, 35–37
*Beneath Wandering Stars* 12, 57, 66–70
Benedis-Grab, Daphne 12, 57, 62, 156; *Army Brats* 12, 57, 62–66
Berg, Elizabeth 2, 13, 89, 108–109, 156; *Durable Goods* 13, 89, 109–112; *Joy School* 13, 89, 109, 112–114; *True to Form* 13, 89, 109, 114–115
Bird, Sarah 13, 89, 115, 156; *The Yokota Officers Club* 13, 89, 115–121
Bohe-Thackwell, Vicki 12, 57, 70; *Too Skinny to Float* 70–71
Bowlby, John 124; *A Secure Base* 124–126, 128, 132, 133, 137
*BRAT and the Kids of Warriors* 12, 80–86
*Brats: Children of the Military Speak Out* 55–56
Bronfenbrenner, Uri 124–125, 128, 132, 133, 137

Cadden, Mike 59
Cerulli, Catherine 61, 155
Chartrand, Malinda M. 4, 154
*Child of the Blue* 12, 20, 37–38
Collins, Carol 62
Collins, Suzanne 13, 102, 123, 127, 143–147; Hunger Games *series* 143, 145–146; *The Year of the Jungle* 143–145
Conroy, Pat 8, 12–13, 20; *The Death of Santini* 12, 20, 38–39; *The Great Santini* 40, 57, 89–98, 109, 113
Coppola, Elizabeth C. 4–6, 153
Cowles, Ashlee 12, 57, 66, 156; *Beneath Wandering Stars* 12, 57, 66–70
Curtis, Mark 12; *Growing Up Military* 45, 48

Davis, Stephen 134–135, 137–140
*The Death of Santini* 12, 20, 38–39
dependent 31, 69, 91, 116
Dominus, Susan 145
Douglas, Kate 12, 17–19
Dowell, Frances O'Roark 12, 57, 75; *Shooting the Moon* 12, 57, 74–77
*Durable Goods* 13, 89, 109–112

Ellis, Deborah 12, 45; *Off to War* 50–55

family violence 6, 18, 24, 28, 31, 34, 38, 47, 53, 61, 84–86, 94, 95, 97–98, 112, 114, 116, 150, 154
flag-lowering ceremony 9, 30, 64, 65, 67

# Index

The Fortres 7, 8, 10, 11, 14–15, 28, 31–32, 35, 38,43, 44, 45, 48–50, 57, 60, 62, 64–65, 70–72, 77, 78–79, 83–84, 86–88, 99, 108–109, 122, 126- 127, 134, 139, 146–147, 153, 156

Gilberg, Gail Hosking 12, 29; *Snake's Daughter* 12, 29–33
Gilmore, Leigh 12, 16–17
Gingrich, Newt 13, 123, 127, 141–147
Goode, Erich 12, 16
*The Great Santini* 40, 57, 89–98, 109, 113
Griffiths, Haley K. 153
Grossman, Dave 41–42
*Growing Up in Khaki* 12
*Growing Up Military* 45, 48
Guzman, Carl 4–5, 152

Hanna, Sandy 20, 25; *The Ignorance of Bliss* 20, 25–29
Harrison, Deborah 45–47, 50–51
Hathaway, Alisa 61, 155
*The Heart of a Shepherd* 12, 76–77
Hubbard, L. Ron 13, 123, 127–133, 141–142, 145–146
Hunger Games series 143, 145–146

*The Ignorance of Bliss* 20, 25–29
*In Country* 13, 89, 99–109
Iraq 4, 5, 32, 42, 55, 58, 76, 78, 149
*The Italian Lesson* 12

*Joy School* 13, 89, 109, 112–114

Kaslow, Florence 150
Kastner, Christine Khira 12; *Soldiering On: Finding My Homes* 12
Kizer, Kenneth W. 151–152

le Menestrel, Suzanne 151–152
Lyons, Michael Joseph 12; *BRAT and the Kids of Warriors* 12, 80–86

Mason, Bobbie Ann 13, 89, 99, 101; *In Country* 13, 89, 99–109; *Patchwork* 99

Medders, Kim 12; *The Italian Lesson* 12
Metzger, Jed 61, 155
*Military Brats: Life Inside the Fortress* 1, 7, 8–11,22, 27, 29, 31, 49, 56, 64, 68, 72–74, 77–78, 81, 84, 96, 99, 109, 113–114, 127
Miller, Russell 127–133
Morrison, Jim 13, 24, 123, 127–129, 131, 133–141, 145–146
moving 1, 21, 26, 36, 38, 48, 55–56, 67, 68, 75,86, 91, 93, 109, 115–116, 124, 126, 128, 139, 142
Murray, Gail 60

*Off to War* 50–55
Osofsky, Joy D. 4, 154

Parry, Roseanne 12, 57, 76; *The Heart of a Shepherd* 12, 76–77
*Patchwork* 99
pets 21, 22, 26, 53, 75, 125
Pollack, Harriet 101
Price, Joanna 99–100, 103, 108
Privitera, Charles R. 6
Prochnicky, Jerry 137–141
Pryce, David H. 149–151
Pryce, Josephine G. 149–151
PTSD 1, 41–42, 47, 100, 144, 150, 155
Purcell, Anne 34, 44, 156: *Love and Duty* 34–35
Purcell, Ben 34, 44, 156: *Love and Duty* 34–35

Riordan, James 137–141
Russotti, Justin 61, 155
Ryan, Diane 12, 20, 37, 44; *Child of the Blue* 12, 20, 37–38

*Saigon Kids* 12, 20–25
Schertz, Kelly 19
*A Secure Base* 124–126, 128, 132, 133, 137
Seltzer, Katherine 39–40, 89–90, 96, 98
Shackleford, Kimberly K. 149–151
Shay, Jonathan 15, 41
Shelton, Lawrence 124

## Index

Shirley, Craig 141–142
*Shooting the Moon* 12, 57, 74–77
Sinor, Jennifer 42–44, 49, 61
Smith, Sidonie 12
*Snake's Daughter* 12, 29–33
*Soldiering On: Finding My Home*s 12
*The Souvenir* 20, 33–34
*Speak Through Me* 12
Steinman, Louise 20, 33; *The Souvenir* 20, 33–34
Stringer, Sharlene 12; *Speak Through Me* 12

theater 9–10, 67, 86
*Too Skinny to Float* 70–71
Townsend, Jasmine A. 153
Tribunella, Eric 61
Trites, Roberta 60, 77
*True to Form* 13, 89, 109, 114–115
Truscott, Mary R. 12, 55; *Brats: Children of the Military Speak Out* 55–56

Vietnam 1, 20–25, 27, 29, 31, 34–35, 41–42, 58, 70–71, 73–74, 89, 99–105, 107–108, 117–119, 140, 142–145, 147, 149

Wadsworth, Shelly MacDermid 4–6, 153
Watson, Cassidy 19
Watson, Jay 102, 106
Watson, Julia 12
Wertsch, Mary Edwards: *Military Brats: Life Inside the Fortress* 1, 7, 8–11, 22, 27, 29, 31, 49, 56, 64, 68, 72–74, 77–78, 81, 84, 96, 99, 109, 113–114, 127
Willis, William 12, 35; *Base Jumping* 12, 35–37
Wright, Lawrence 127–128, 131, 133

*The Year of the Jungle* 143–145
*The Yokota Officers Club* 13, 89, 115–121

www.ingramcontent.com/pod-product-compliance
Lightning Source LLC
Chambersburg PA
CBHW032048300426
44117CB00009B/1231